THE TUNNE
or
"EL CAMINO VASC(
or
"VÍA DE B?

CU01507863

HENDAYE to SANTO DOMINGO de la CALZADA and BURGOS

By Tony Roberts

PREFACE

It was in 1997, unbeknown to each other at the time, that Eric Walker and I, our appetites whetted by John Durant's article in the Confraternity of St James' *Bulletin* of February 1995, decided to explore this route. Eric Walker cycled the route and I completed it on foot. We carried only Michelin road maps and the two guidebooks, *Dos Caminos a Santiago* and *Por Álava a Compostela*, which had been published in 1993 and 1992 respectively.

Both were good on background information, but they were not written in English, dealt only with those sections of the Camino within the three Basque provinces and were insufficiently detailed adequately to describe the off-road paths to which they referred.

These shortcomings prompted Eric to return to Spain in 1998 to walk some of those sections of the route that he had been unable to travel on his bicycle.

It was his intention to produce a series of guidebooks covering inter alia: -

1), "El Camino del Norte" or "Camino de la Costa" from Hendaye, via Bilbao, Gijon and Ribadeo to Arzua,

2), "El Camino Primitivo del Interiór" from Villaviciosa, via Oviedo and Lugo, to Palas del Rey and

3), this route, "El Camino Vasco del Interiór," ("Via de Bayona") which we popularly know as the "The Tunnel Route," because it passes through St Adrian's Tunnel in the Sierra de Urquilla on its way to the plains of Álava.

Eric had already compiled a brief outline guide for the "Tunnel Route" but, having learned that I had walked the whole route, he sent it to me for comment.

Having discovered many alterations in the route when I walked the route again with my companion, Judith Leigh, in September 2000, I accepted the task of writing an up-to-date guide. The first Tunnel Route Guide was published by the Confraternity of St James in 2002.

This current edition of the Guide is based on my findings along those stretches of Camino I have been able to visit over the past year and on feedback gratefully received in respect of other parts. Unfortunately, I have not been able to rewalk the whole of the route, so apologies are tendered for any current discrepancy.

This guide will be out of date by the time it is published, and I and the publishers accept no liability for any information found to be incorrect at the time of its use.

The accuracy of any guide relies primarily upon feedback from those who have used it. Any additional information, and/or details of any appropriate amendment or correction, which would enable this guide to be kept up to date, would be appreciated. Such information can be forwarded either to The Confraternity or directly to me (see contact details on P55).

Tony Roberts, March 2010

The historic approach to Hendaye

Many pilgrims from the north crossed the mouth of the Gironde to the Pointe de Grave and then made their way South by following the coastal route via St Vincent de Tyrosse (on the **N-10**) and then through Ondres, Tarnos and St Esprit de Bayonne to St Jean-de-Luz. In St Jean-de-Luz they walked round the bay to Socoa to find the preferred route to Hendaye along *la Crête des Collines*. This roughly corresponds to the present day road that turns inland from Socoa and passes through Kalitcho, travelling up the valley of the R. Ruisseau (Unxin-(B)). The route gradually edged up the northern slopes of the valley to reach the ridge, which it then followed, before descending through Orio to reach Hendaye (Hendaia (B)) itself.

Here, pilgrims had the problem of crossing the wide Río Bidasoa, into Spain.

On the banks of the Bidasoa in Hendaye was situated the Monastery or Priory of Zubernoa (Subernoa-(C)). This not only provided a pilgrim hospital, the Priory-Hospital of Santiago (Note--Santiago **not** Saint Jacques although still in France), but also, as was recorded in the 13th century, a boat service, which crossed the river to arrive at the old Roman port area of Irún (now, the *barrio de Santiago*). Later, a wooden bridge built by the Prior crossed the main channel of the river to one of the *joncaux*, (a large, low-lying, reed covered island). Pilgrims were then able to make their way across the adjoining *joncaux* to reach the opposite bank.

Present day pilgrims can just about follow the route early pilgrims took through Hendaye, by leaving **Orio** via the **Rue d'Orio** and turning left into the **Boulevard de l'Empereur.** Follow the boulevard, and continue straight ahead along the **Rue des Réservoirs** to the crossroads, where the road to the right, the **Rue de Irandatz,** is followed to the next major road junction. At this junction the **Rue de Santiago** is taken. This is followed until, nearer the river, the **Rue Priorenia** can be found leading down to the river.

The name Priorenia is our clue to the sites of the former Priory of Subernoa's Hospital de Santiago and the church of St Jacques de Zubernoa, which were destroyed by the Spanish Invasion under General Ventura Caro in 1793. The one remaining relic from the church is the baptismal font, which today is sited in the Parish Church of St Vincent in the centre of Hendaye.

In 1801 the lands were bought on behalf of Etienne Pellot, a notorious corsair who had the large house, the Priorenia, built there for his eventual retirement.

In 1813, when the area was under the occupation of the British, the Duke of Wellington visited the house, the war damage to which, by then, had been repaired by, and at the expense of the British. Today, very little remains of it.

The modern route from the Gironde to Hendaye, via Bayonne, is now covered by the Confraternity's **Pilgrim's Guide to the Roads through France No 5 – "La Voie Littorale"** by Judy Smith.

LOCATION MAP

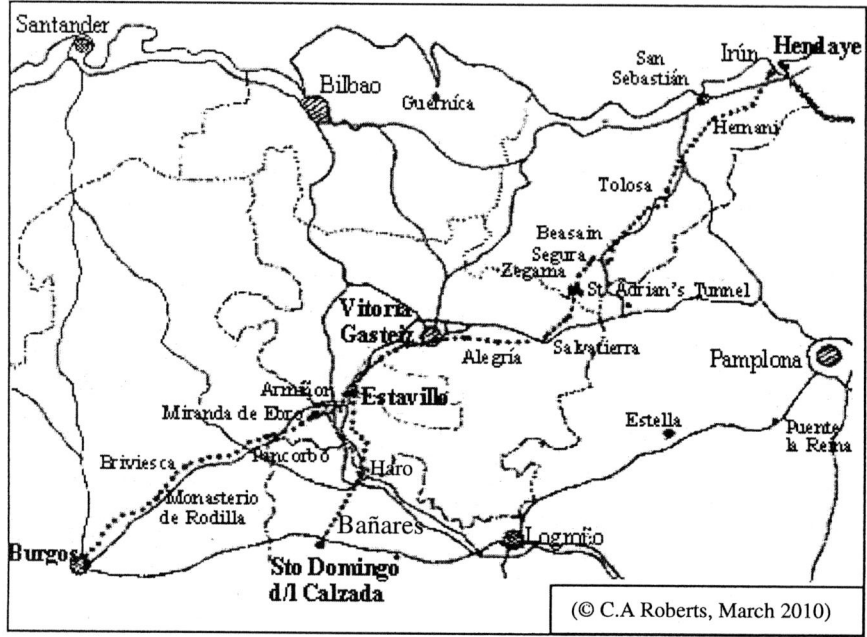

(© C.A Roberts, March 2010)

"El Camino Vasco del Interiór" otherwise known **"Vía de Bayona"** or **"The Tunnel Route,"** starts in Hendaye near Irún, a border town in the NE corner of the Basque province of Gipuzkoa. It and the **"Camino de la Costa"** (or **"Camino del Norte"**), form natural continuations of the **"Voie Littorale,"** the route from the Gironde (via Bayonne) to Hendaye.

It winds over wooded hills to Hernani and Urnieta before following the narrow, high-sided but commercialised valley of the Rio Oria to Beasain. It then becomes more and more rural as it passes the ancient towns of Segura and Cegama. It continues through woods up to and beyond St Adrian's Tunnel and descends to the flatter fields of Álava Province, where it traces its way along the *Camino de los Romanos* towards Vitoria. From Vitoria, rural roads and tracks are followed through undulating and sometimes hilly countryside to Estavillo. Here, the route divides into: -

1) The route through the Rioja vineyards and the Ebro valley, via Briñas, Haro and Bañares, to join the *Camino Francés* in **Sto Domingo de la Calzada,** and

2) The route via Armiñón, Miranda de Ebro, Pancorbo, Briviesca and Monasterio de Rodillo to join the *Camino Francés* in **Gamonál (Burgos).**

From **Hendaye,** it is approximately 200kms to **Sto Domingo de la Calzada** and approximately 260kms to **Burgos.**

STAGE / DISTANCE PLANNER

Place	Acco m?	Dist. in Kms Alt've	Dist. in Kms Main	Stage Distance
Hendaye	Yes		0.00	
Irun	Yes		1.40	
Gurutze	Yes		7.50	
Oiartzun	Yes		2.20	
Astigarraga	Yes		13.75	
Hernani	Yes		3.25	
Urnieta	Yes		2.80	
Andoain	Yes		4.60	
Villabona	Yes		5.30	
Anoeta	Yes		3.90	
Tolosa	Yes		3.00	
Legorreta	Yes		11.65	
Itsasondo	Yes		3.00	
Beasain	Yes	⌐	4.00	
Olaberria	Yes	↓	3.00	
Idiazabal	Yes	↓	3.70	
Segura	Yes	7.40	3.75	
Cegama	Yes	7.90	5.50	
Tunnel	Yes		7.50	
Zalduondo	No		8.20	
Salvatierra	Yes		6.00	
Alegria (turn off pt)	Yes		10.40	
Estíbaliz (turn off pt)	Yes		5.90	
Arcaya	Yes	⌐	8.70	
Vitoria	Yes	↓	4.00	
Arméntia	No	6.20	3.00	
Subijana	Yes		7.15	
La Puebla de Arg'zón	Yes	9.00	8.80	
Berantevilla	Yes		11.90	
Salinillas de Buradón	Yes		9.45	
Briñas	Yes		4.75	
Haro	Yes		3.75	
Sto Domingo d/l C	Yes		19.50	
TOTAL			**201.30**	**To BURGOS – 259kms**

5

INTRODUCTION

General comment

Waymarking along the route is generally good. It is provided in the form of wooden wayside markers, wooden finger posts, painted metal angle iron posts and various methods of ground level signing including the yellow arrow.

An area of exception lies to the east of Vitoria, where huge scale road and other development works have been ongoing over the last two years or so. The work impinges on the routes which, up till now, have given passage to pilgrims. However, it is clear that a new routing for pilgrims through the city centre is included in the overall plan, and waymarkers have already been provided along the Puerto de Elorriaga, the Paseo de Santiago, through the Old Town and out along the several Paseos to Armentia. Camino leaflets from the Tourist Office indicate that a link between Arcaya and Elorriaga is envisaged but, clearly, it is too early to waymark it.

Currently, the new routing can only be accessed, in any practicable manner, from Askartza/Ascarza by way of the very busy A-132/N-130 and N-104 roads.

I am not aware of any proposals to alter or do away with the City Centre bypass route from Arcaya, (described in *Por Alava a Compostella* and *Dos Caminos a Santiago),* so I have attempted to describe currently practicable versions of the two routes from Arcaya.

All sections of the walking pilgrims' route, which are considered to be unsuitable for cyclists, are dealt with in the **Section for Cyclists.**

Note on place names and maps

Where they are known, both the Basque (B) and the equivalent Castilian (C) place names are given. The name believed to be in more common use, is given first, and its equivalent is given, in brackets, second.

The Michelin Roadmap No 442 is quite helpful in that you can locate the route within its wider surroundings, but the best maps to use are the IGN maps which can be viewed at scales of up to 1/20000, together with even larger scale satellite pictures, on www.sigpac.mapa.es/fega/visor.

Note on language

Although the Route takes you through the Basque Country, you will find that you will not be expected to speak *Euskera*, and that *Castellano* is an accepted means of communication. However, the *Euskadek (Vascos)* are justifiably proud of their heritage, and if you were to use only one or two Basque words, they would appreciate your recognition of their language. Accordingly, a short glossary of hopefully useful Basque words is given at the end of this guidebook.

Note on accommodation
This route does not yet have the full pilgrim Refugio / Albergue infrastructure of the Camino Francés, and. pilgrims have to rely chiefly on the Hotel / Agroturismo / Casa Rural network. Since beds in these establishments may in relatively short supply, it might be appropriate to ring ahead to confirm availability. It is necessary to ring ahead to arrange accommodation in the few refugios that have been opened during the last few years.
Accommodation costs are generally 50% higher in the Pais Vasco than in other parts of North Spain. You should budget accordingly, and, perhaps, travel in twos or fours if you want to keep costs down.

General guide to abbreviations

H*	Hotel, one star
HR*	Hotel Residencia, one star (No restaurant)
HS*/HS**	Hostal one / two star
HSR*/HSR**	Hostal Residencia, one / two star (No restaurant)
R/H	Restaurant/Hostal
F/P	Fonda / Pension
A/T	Agroturismo (Nekazalturismoa), (Farm / Guesthouse)
C/R	Casas Rurales, (Country Homes)
Alb Mun	Albergue Municipal (Municipal Hostel)
Ref	Refugio de Peregrinos (Pilgrim Refuge)

Approximate prices in January / February 2009
€

H**/***	55/90 per dbl rm per nt	Inc IVA	With bathroom
HR/HSR**	40/60 p.d.r.p.n.	Inc IVA	With bathroom
H*, P and F	35/50 p.d.r.p.n.	Inc IVA	With bathroom
P and F	30/45 p.d.r.p.n.	Inc IVA	Share bathroom
A/T)	35/60 p.d.r.p.n.	Exc IVA	With bathroom
C/R)			

Differential high/low season rates may apply. "High season" is normally from say 1 May to 8 September, but sometimes only from 1 July to 31 August.
Some establishments may be prepared to allow pilgrims some reduction in the room charge. It will not hurt to make a polite enquiry.
Even though brochures might indicate that some A/Ts and C/Rs do not provide breakfasts and evening meals, it is always worthwhile asking about their availability. Efforts are sometimes made to help those on foot, who are "passing through." Use of a kitchen is also a possibility.

Albergues (Aterpeak)

While these exist in several towns, they were not provided primarily for the use of pilgrims. They are akin to the English Youth Hostel and are often prebooked for parties of children on organised activity outings. You are advised to telephone, prior to the day of arrival, to explain your situation as a Santiago pilgrim and, hopefully, attempts will be made to find accommodation for you.

ACCOMMODATION LIST - Hendaye to Sto Domingo de la Calzada

Irún:

HSR**	Irún, Zubiaurre 5,	943 612283
HSR**	Lizaso,Aduana,5-7	943 611600
HS**	Machinvente, Paseo de Colon, 21	943 621384
P**	Los Fronterizos, Estación, 7	943 619205
P**	Bidasoa, Estacion 14	943 619913
Ref	C/Lucas de Berroa 18. Open 16:00 to 22:00	?

Gurutze

HR*	Gurutze Berri	943 490625

Oiartzun

A/T	Arri Gain, Iturriotz, 20180, Oiartzun.	943 491104
Camping Oliden (4.5km off route)		943 490728
	Madrid / Irún Road, Km 476.	

Errenteria

A/T	Anarre Zarre, Zamalbide Zona, Errentaria	943 523751

Astigarraga

A/T	Arraspine, Santiago Mendi, 20115, Astigarraga	943 331319
A/T	Artola, Santiago Mendi, 20115, Astigarraga	(943 557296
		(637 035679
C/R	Buenavista, Ermana Berri, 2	943 330205

Hernani

P	Zinko Enea, Kale Nagusia 57-1	670 390897
P	Txoko, (unstaffed)	(608 770602
		(943 557557

Urnieta

A/T	Montefrio, Goiburu Bailara	943 557158
P**	Villa de Urnieta, C/Dendategi 4.	943 333866

Aduna

R/H	Benta Jatetxea, Barrio Elbarrena	943 693094
A/T	Zabale, Goiburu, 20150 Aduna	943 690825

Villabona

A/T	Alustiza, Amasa	943 690361
A/T	Urresti, Amasa	943 690444

8

Tolosa

	Albergue Municipal, off Hernialde Rd	943 650036
H	Hostal Oyarbide, Plaza Gorriti, 1	943 670017
P	Karmentxu, Korreo 24	943 673701
H	Urrutitxo, Kondeko Aldapa, 7	943 673822

Legorreta

R/H	Hostal Izarra, Ctra. Nacional-1, No16	943 806044

Itsasondo

H**	Izaskun, Kale Nagusia, 13	943 880012

Beasain

H**	Igartza, Oriamendi Kalea, 41A	943 085240
H*	Salbatore, Barrio Salbatore	943 888307
A/T	Lizargarate, 20210 Lazkao	943 881974
	(3km off route)	

Olaberria

H**	Zezilione, Herriko Plaza, Olaberria	943 885829
A/T	Borda, Errekalde	943 160681
	(4.5km off road route, and 1.5km off scenic route)	

Idiazabal

R/H	Zepai Jatetxea, 20213, Idiazabal	(943 187723
		(943 187198

Segura

A/T	Ondarre Baserria, 20214 Segura	943 801664

Zegama

HS*	Ostatu Jatetxea, Zegama	943 801051
A/T	Arrieta Haundi	943 801890
	(Transport from and to Zegama by arrangement)	
C/R	Dinti Barrena	943 421958
	Refuge	943 802187

St Adrian's Tunnel

	Alb. Municpal.	943 582076

Salvatierra

CH	Jose Mari, C / Mayor 73	945 300042
CH	Merino, Pza de San Juan, 3	945 300052
	Albergue de las Claretianos	945 300214
	Albergue de las Clarisas	945 300062

Alegria-Dulantzi

P**	Antolin, Fortaleza 9,	(945 420328
	Refuge Ronzapil	945 420027

Santuario de Estíbaliz

	Refuge	(945 293088

Arcaya

Refuge	CasadeEspiritualidad.Leku	?

Vitoria/Gasteiz

H**	Dato C/Eduardo Dato 28	945 147230
H/S**	Florida, Manuel Iradier, 33.	945 260675
H/R*	Amarica, C/ Florida, 11.	945 130506
H/R*	Achuri/Atxuri, Rioja, 11.	945 255800
P**	Araba, C/ Florida, 25.	945 232588
YH	AJ Carlos Arbaitua, C/ Escultor Isaac Diez	945 299914
	Open 16:00 to 22:00	

Subijana

H***	Ruta de Europa, (1.7km off route on N-1)	945 361416

La Puebla de Arganzón

HR**	Arganzón Plaza, Plaza Mayor 2	(945 373470
		(629 504370
HS**	Los Palacios, Ctra Madrid / Irún, Km333	945 373030
HS*/P.	Pili, Ctra Mad'd / Irún, Km334	945 373088
Refuge	C/ Cercas 6 Tel Town Hall 0900 – 1400	945 373006

Berantevilla

Refuge	Centro Social	?

Salinillas de Buradón

A/T,	Areta Etxea, C / Mayor, 17	(945 274757
		(941 337275
Pte Refuge	La Bodega Aterpea	657 735034

Briñas

H/R	Portal de la Rioja,	941 311480

Haro

P.	La Pena, C / La Vega, 1-2nd.	(941 304101?
		(941 310022?
P.	Aragon, C/La Vega 9.	941 310004
Refuge	Calle Juan Carlos I, 23	(677 321806
		(627 602124

Santo Domingo

See Pilgrim Guide No 1-"The Camino Francés"

ACOMMODATION LIST - Estavillo to Burgos

Miranda de Ebro

Albergue Juvenil Fernán Gonzáles, C/ Anduva 82	947 320932

Pancorbo
Albergue Parroquial, C/ Real 21, (Ask the Parish Priest) ?
Briviesca
Pensión Casa Cuevas, Avda Félix Rodríguez, 11 947 592079
Monasterio de Rodillo
HR Picon del Conde. 947 594355
La Brújula
HR La Brújula, N-1. 947 430391
Burgos
See Pilgrim Guide No 1-"The Camino Francés"

PART I - THE WALKERS' ROUTE

Normal script.....................Waymarked Routes
Italic script.........................Alternative Routes

PART I (A) - HENDAYE to ESTAVILLO

International Bridge (Puente de Santiago), Hendaye **0.0 km**
Shops, hostels, bars.

From **Hendaye Ville** railway station, make your way to and over the **International Bridge**. Follow the cycle track in front of the parade of shops for 100m and go left around the roundabout you come to on Avda de Iparralde. You will spot the first waymarkers at ground-level only a few metres on the left beyond the roundabout. This is the start of both the **Camino del Norte (Camino de la Costa)** and the **Camino Vasco del Interiór**. If you still want to 'do' the Tunnel Route, turn left to access the **Paseo del Real Unión** along the river. After passing under a main road, leave the river and go along **Calle Santiago Kalea**, towards Church of Nuestra Señora del Juncal, which is visible at its end. Go to the left of the church as you approach it and turn to the right around it, up the steps and onwards to the **Paseo de Colón**. This is the main shopping street of Irún and in it, or just off it, it is possible to find lodgings. If you want to go to the Refuge, follow Colón to the right, turn right immediately after you cross the main railway lines and turn second left at a minor roundabout into Lucas Berroa. Otherwise, cross the road into the Plaza de San Juan where, beyond the car parks, you will see the *Casa Consistoriál or* Town Hall of

Irún. **1.40 km**
Full facilities. Pilgrim Refuge – open 1600hrs to 2200hrs (21 beds & Kit, Credenciales and Sello available).

Most of the town was destroyed by fire during the Civil War, but, as is now obvious, has been rebuilt.

In the C15th Church of Santa Maria de Juncal, is a black Virgin and Child dating from the 12th century (venerated by both mariners and pilgrims of old). There is also a 13th century Processional Crucifix.

Close to it, used to be a pilgrims' hospital dedicated to Santa Margarita, which the French destroyed in 1638.

In the town's outskirts is the fountain and hermitage of St Elena built on the remains of a former Roman Temple.

Head for the road passing to the right of the Town Hall, Leon Iruratagoiena Kalea. On the right, just beyond the car park, alongside a bar and about 50m before you reach the Town Hall, you will find Nagusia Kalea/Calle Mayor. Follow this and veer left into Calle Artaleku. This will lead you to Avda de Gipuzkoa, where, almost opposite you, is a large filling station fronting on to a roundabout. Go through the filling station to find ahead of you the exit from the roundabout taking you uphill along Avda de Elizatxo. After going straight ahead at a smaller roundabout, look on your left for Calle de Belitz and follow it over the Autopista. At a bend about 100m up the ensuing rise, take the first (cement) track to the right. It is now downhill to a left turn at the bottom before you swing right between two houses. Follow the earth track through woodland and use a narrow bridge to cross a stream. Go left after the stream ultimately to reach a cement road. Here, go straight ahead keeping a house on your left, to access a green track. This leads you past a waste factory and to a driveway taking you to the GI-3451/ GI-3452, where you turn right.

After a double S-bend, you come to a point where the road makes a sharp bend to the right (north). Here, you will see straight ahead, a cement surfaced track.

Turn left off the road and follow the track up past a scrap yard on the left and past a farm on your right. On more level ground amongst trees at the top of the ensuing rise, go straight over a junction with other tracks, and then, as you continue forwards, you will get a clear view of Gurrutze and the route ahead.

A steep descent followed by a short but equally steep ascent brings you out at a roundabout opposite two convenient bars, and close to the Hotel at

Gurrutze.   **7.5 km**
Bars, Accommodation.

Turn left to follow the main (GI-2134) road for 50m, and then turn right to walk downhill on a local road. You swing left down to a track which follows a stream before veering left and rising to reach a cemented track. Keep following this track up and round to the left as others join you from the right. You will come to a wider local road rising steeply from the main road down to your left. Turn right to follow it through the woods and ignore a left turn down to some houses. Just after this, take a left fork to descend steeply down Calle San Juan Kalea, past several stone crosses, to its junction with the town centre bypass road on the northeast side of

Oiartzun (Elizalde-(C)).   **2.2 km**
Shops, Bars, Clinic, Buses, Accommodation.
Roman mines and pre-Christian burial mounds can be found in the area.

On the opposite right hand corner of the crossroads you have just reached is a bus stop and the emblazoned *Casa de Cultura*, formerly the Hospital of St John, in which there is a Tourist Information Office, a Library and a Museum. You can obtain a sello from the Library on the 1st floor.

Continue down over the crossroads and past the Library and the 16th century Church of San Estéban beyond it, which has a 17th century altar. Behind it used to stand the Chapel of the Hospital of St John. A few metres more will bring you into the Plaza Mayor. Do not go left into the Plaza, but keep straight on and slightly right to find **Manuel Lekuona Etorbidea** (opposite a handy bar), which leads immediately left off the exit road at the South West corner of the Plaza. By ignoring all side turnings, this road will eventually take you across the Rio Oiartzun to the **Iturrioz** district, where you will come out to the right of another roundabout and opposite a small park.
Go up the steps to the left of the small park and continue straight on along the road ahead of you for about 400m where you will swing round to the right past an animal sanctuary and an ornamental (not drinking water) fountain. After another 350m, you will see straight ahead of you 'caserio' **Estrataburu**, which may be partially hidden behind some trees. The road veers left here to pass A/T Arri Gain, but you take the right turn immediately after passing Estrataburu.
At the bottom of this local road, your route is signed left down a track to a watersmeet, which you cross by means of two small bridges. 50m further on, you fork right steeply up a hill, and, when you reach more open ground at the top, you veer left to follow the rear boundary fence of a house. Follow this fence round to the right until it debouches onto the concrete road onto which the house fronts. You follow this road to the left and then almost immediately fork left up a rise to a house. This leads you to a green track which brings you to a road along which you turn left to reach a T-junction on the Esnao Soro ridge.
Here, you will see, straight ahead of you, a view of the valley you are going to cross, and the track you are about to follow. It leads along a fence on the right and an orchard on the left, bears right at the end of the fence and goes down and across a meadow. It bears left through woods and down and right to a farm.

13

Turn hard left to exit the farmyard and follow the drive to its junction with a road. Turn right along it for 50m or so to a T-junction with another road on the other side of a stream, which is bridged by two parallel pieces of concrete.

Straight opposite you is a field entrance, which gives onto a track going up left past a deserted building before it reaches another road. Turn right along this road, follow it for about 300m and then turn left up a concrete track signposted to **Anarre Zarra** (A/T), which you pass before reaching, on your right, **Oiarzabal Baserria Orereta**. At this point, you leave the concrete track for an earth track, which skirts woodland before it enters a corner of it. Here, there is a confluence of tracks, but go diagonally right to continue ahead along a wider track alongside a fence coincident with a local trail marked with white and yellow flashes. Continue following this track until you come to an electricity pylon, which you pass on its left and continue straight on to a bar in **Listoreta** 150m further on. Exit the car park and follow the road south for another 150m or so to find your right turn.

This leads down into the valley (steeply in places) and you follow the track ignoring all side turnings until you reach the bar/restaurant (closed on Wednesdays) about 100m before reaching the Ventas to Astigárraga road in

Frantzesillaga.   **8.0 km**
Bar / Restaurant.

Turn right along this road and after a few metres you will see an open area on your left accommodating a *Probadero* (a cobbled area c.23m long x 6m wide, where the strength of pairs of bulls is tested in a form of time trial, by having them drag a large, extremely heavy piece of rock over the cobbles). Turn left here and follow the well-defined track to merge with another track coming from your left. This track leads you to a farmhouse, just beyond which is a crossroads. Your route is the road going to the right. The road swings left as it passes a track going off to the right (which you ignore) and then reaches an entrance to a seemingly disused compound on your left. As you reach this entrance, you will see ahead of you, an earth track (surfaced at first with broken terracotta tiles). Follow it up and around the hill until it emerges onto a concrete road. Turn right along it for about 90m and take the left fork up to a T-junction 15m ahead of you.

At the T-junction you will see a road leading to some houses and a stony path to its right rising directly opposite you. Follow this up the hill and onward to a circular car park/turning area. To the right of this is a track, which leads you to the summit of Santiomendi, and the **Ermita de Santiago** with its **Refuge** facility (sadly, I have no information as to how to gain access). On a good day, you can delight in the splendid panorama, the picnic benches and the fountain available here.

14

Follow the tarmacked road down from the Ermita past the entrance to the parking area and past the end of Ermita Bidea. Immediately after this, turn left to follow the road serving the radio repeater station, the house and the two disused cottages above you. Having passed the two cottages, the road peters out into a descending earth track. Keep straight on where it forks left up to the radio station and follow the downward slope for about 250m to come to where you are directed to the right along a very uneven narrow grass and stone path. This swings down to the right, ultimately to join a cement residential road serving **Txapa Borda**. Turn left down this road and right at the next junction near **Buenavista (C/R)**. This will take you down to **Artola Nekazalturismoa** and its **Sagardotegia** at the junction with **Iraultza Bidea**. From here, it is about 4.6km into Hernani, if you follow the waymarking or 3.6km **via a short cut (see later.)**

Follow Iraultza to the right for 50m or so and you will reach **Nekazalturismoa Arraspine Baserria** where a badly placed waymark on the back wall of the Baserria directs you left behind the house, down through the fields and past a *Monastegia* to **Astigárraga**. When you reach the next road, follow it round to the right and then go left down a hill before joining the road from Oiartzun (Elizalde). Turn left, and after a few more metres you will merge with the main Donostia (San Sebastián (C)) to Hernani road. Go left and very shortly, on your left, you will take the service road, which at first runs parallel to the main road, before connecting with a quieter road which will take you left into the **Ergobia** District. It will take you along **Oialume Bidea**, past the **Gurutzeta Sagardotegia** and a road going off to the left where there are direction notices for the above-mentioned Artola Baserria and Buenavista.

*To take advantage of the shorter route, turn left around Artola instead of going right, and, at the next T-junction, turn right. Follow it down to **Oialume Bidea** where you turn left along the waymarked route.*

Follow **Oialume Bidea** into **Mikel Arozamena Bidea,** and swing right to a T-junction where you go right before swinging left to rejoin the Donostia / Hernani road at a double roundabout system. Follow the footpath across the 1st roundabout and go under the high level bypass road. Cross the next roundabout and follow the road towards Hernani.

Here we have alternative routes. The waymarked route continues along the main road directly into Hernani. If you take this route, look out for Bar Txoko (for access to Pension Txoko) before you walk up C/Nagusia to the Plaza Mayor.

If you want to bypass Hernani, follow the other route thus. 50m towards Hernani from the 2nd roundabout, turn left along an unwaymarked path/road leading into the **Akerregi** industrial estate. Take the next turning to the right along the estate's central road. Coming out of the estate, you will go straight over a roundabout, then over the "old" River Urumea Bridge before reaching a junction, where the road left is indicated as **Portu Auzoa,** and some apartment blocks stand immediately in front of you.

*Here you can either go into **Hernani** or continue your bypass by turning left to follow a road parallel to the river on your left, through the barrio known as **El Puerto** (so called, because it was the highest point to which the river was once navigable).*
Follow it for about 500m, after which, you will see on your right, just before you cross a small bridge over a stream, a large house standing on what is a large triangular traffic island (to the right and behind it is a bar). Immediately over the bridge, a waymarker directs you to the right alongside the stream.
It is at this point that you meet the waymarked route out of Hernani

If you decide to go into the town, go straight on to Hernani Railway Station via the service road accessing the apartment blocks. Your route takes you under the railway, to the left and then to the right up a multi-flight of steps, across a road, through an arch and along an alley into the old part of the town, where a yellow arrow sends you (left) up one of the narrow streets into the Plaza Mayór of

Hernani.   **8.75 km**
Railway, Buses, Shops, Banks, Bars, Restaurants, Accommodation, Police Station for advice and sello, Chemist.

From the Plaza Mayór, go through the archway at its southeast corner and look for the waymarker pointing you down steps to your left. These will take you down to a road which will take you under the railway and on to the bridge over the stream in **Portu Auzoa/El Puerto** (see above). Turn right immediately after the bridge to parallel the stream and, at the end of this short road, look for the narrow uphill opening between the last houses on the left. Follow this track and you will eventually join a road coming from the left, close to Urnieta Station and, not long afterwards, you reach a road-bridge over the railway, leading into

Urnieta.   (from centre of Hernani) **2.8 km**
Bar, Trains, Shops, Accommodation.

The waymarked route is straight ahead past some factory buildings on the left. After 400m you will reach another bridge over the railway on your right, where you are rejoined by the above alternative route.
 Keep straight on and turn right along a path bordering a heavy vehicle parking area close to a Kaiko milk products plant. At the end of the path, go up the steps, turn right along the road for 50m and take a paved track hard left to

double back on yourself. This rises gradually up and round to the left and then round to the right to join a service road in front of some commercial premises. 75m down this road, turn left on the far side of a municipal (?) vehicle depot down and along a track which will lead you to a service road in front of more commercial premises about 300m distant.

Follow this service road parallel to the GI-131 to its end, where a turning to the left will lead to a footpath up to the bed of a former railway. Go to the right and through the old tunnel, follow the paved track to a road leading you forward to a roundabout, and bear right to face the Church of St Martin of Tours in

Andoain. 4.6 km
Café / bars, Shops, Buses, Trains, Accommodation, Chemist.

If you cannot obtain a sello at St Martin's Church, you can do so at the Police Station, next door to the Church, where you can also get information about local facilities.

Turn left in front of St Martin's Church, and follow the waymarked route along side roads parallel to the River Oria, before turning right to cross it on the road leading to Villabona. This is a busy road and you should proceed with caution as you follow it under a motorway and round, left, eventually to pass Benta Jatetxea, (with some accommodation), and one or two roads off to the right to Aduna. (where you can turn right if you intend to stay at the A/T in Aduna). After about 1km more, you will arrive at a T-junction. Here, at the northern end of the Aduna Bridge, go right to access a rest / picnic area. The Way lies along the road around the rest area taking you directly into the centre of

Villabona. 5.3 km
Bars, Restaurants, Shops, Railway Station, Health Centre.

On reaching a T-junction with roundabout in the centre of the town, you will see a bar opposite, and, diagonally left, a church with clock and bell tower. Follow the road under the railway bridge to the left of the church, cross a secondary watercourse, and you will come to the main bridge over the River Oria itself. Do not cross the river, but turn right along a neighbourhood road / walkway parallel to it, and through the suburb of Ubera. (There is a bar on the right along here).

Continue on past a children's play area on your left, and join the road, which comes over the river from your left. It swings left and you follow it straight ahead, parallel to the railway lines on your right.

Eventually, after about 2km, this road will take you over a level crossing and become narrower. Continue to follow it. It passes back under the railway and runs not far from the river before turning right under a brick railway arch.

Almost immediately, you come to an urban thoroughfare where you turn left and follow the road up the hill to join San Juan Kale. Here you turn for central

Anoeta.   **3.9 km**
Bars, Restaurants, Buses, Railway Station, Shops,

Just after a bar on your right and a restaurant on your left, you reach a bridge over the railway. Don't cross it, but take the road to Hernialde to the right. Follow this for about 500m before turning left to pass under a low bridge under the railway. Turn right along the now only moderately used former main road and follow it parallel to the Oria to

Tolosa.   **3.0 km**
Café / bars, Restaurants, Accommodation, Railway Station, Buses, Shops, Town Hall and Police Station for sello, Chemist.

When you reach the bridge over the R Oria, carry straight on over the small Plaza de Filipe Gorriti and follow the street furthest left – Emperadore/Agintari – to the Church of Santiago in Plaza Andre Maria. Continue on down Emperadore to the River but do not cross the bridge. Turn to the right of the covered market along Zerkania Kalea and, at its end, go past or through the Arch. 40m after the Arch and on your left, look for and follow a wide passageway under the buildings leading to the river. Turn right along the river to follow Zumalakarregi Ibiltokia and on past the bullring. Turn left over the very next bridge and right immediately after it to follow the walkway along the river past the football ground. Keep following the river until you come to a tributary which forces the path left and leads you to a footbridge over the tributary. Cross the footbridge towards a large sports complex. A Camino direction arrow on the corner of the complex may point to the left. Ignore it and go right to follow a tarmacced track along the river in front of an area ready for redevelopment. This track will bring you to a road going under the N-1 above you to your left. Go under the bridge, and after it, turn right along a new pedestrian/cyclist way which you will follow, ultimately to link with the GI-2131 (old N-1) into

Alegia (Alegria de Oria(C))   **5.90 km**
Shops, Cobbler, Bar/Restaurants, Trains, Buses, Chemist.

Your way lies along the central thoroughfare of this old town, past the shops and church, and back onto the GI-2131, which you follow to **Icazteguieta** and

Legorreta.   **5.75 km**
Shops, Bars, Post Office, Accommodation, Chemist, Information Office.

Just before Legorreta, at a point where the main road starts to climb to cross the railway, your route moves left off the GI-2131 and onto a local road. The local road crosses the railway track and a river, before bringing you to the far side of the town centre, where you turn left along the main street. You are now, once again, on the GI-2131, which you will continue following to

Itsasondo (Isasondo (C)).   **3.0 km**
Bar/Restaurants, Accommodation.

About 500m after Itsasondo, just before the road sweeps up and round to the left to cross over the railway and link with the new N-1, you must take the GI-4761 road to the right, which is signposted to

Villafranca de Ordizia / Ordizia.   **2.0 km**
Bars, Restaurant, Shops, no accommodation.

Go straight over the crossroads by the memorial and the patioed bars, and on up a narrower street past the Police Station in the town centre. Keep following this road. It will lead you along the west bank of the Oria, and into the centre of

Beasain.   **2.0 km**
Shops, Café / bars, Restaurants, Railway Station, Town Hall / Police Station for sello and assistance. Accommodation, Post Office, Chemist.

From Beasain to Segura, you have a choice of routes.

1) The Scenic Route via Olaberria and Idiazabal (Not suitable for cyclists)

Having entered Beasain along Kale Nagusia and gone as far as the Police Station in the Market Hall arcade, which is on your right under a bandstand, turn left opposite the far end of the arcade and go down the pedestrian precinct and across the river bridge. You will then be at a road junction, where the GI-120 road leads off (opposite you) to Lazkao via an underpass under the railway and the N-1. Follow this road to the far end of the underpass, and turn right up the slip road to the N-1 for San Sebastián.
After a few metres you will turn left up a road signed to I.E.Institutoa and waymarked with white and yellow flashes and a red cyclist, which denotes a "sporting" route for unladen mountain bikes.
The road soon changes to a narrow concrete track and swings to the left as it climbs towards a farm on the left. On the right just before the farm, is a gate marked "Camino Particular" with the yellow and white blazes of the local trail

on its right hand post. Pass through the gate, and climb the zigzag road to the top of the ridge. From the large house on your right, the route continues straight ahead, but now along a gravel track and its earth track extension. Follow this without deviation to where it veers right away from the woods and meets a distinct rural road. Turn hard left along it and keep straight on in front of Caserio Garitain, when its access drive forks to the right. Once past the Caserio, a tarmacked surface will take you directly to the Plaza Mayor in

Olaberria.   **3.0 km**
Hotel / Restaurant / Bars, Fountain, 17th century Church of San Juan Bautista.

Turn right between the hotel and the Church and follow the S-bend down to a roundabout. Here, the waymarked route goes right and follows the road downhill for about 500m before branching off left up into the fields and leading you thence to an Information Board in **Oyarbide**. However, the more direct route is to cross straight over the roundabout and take the fairly narrow road, which leads off between a house on the left and a larger bar/restaurant on the right. Take the left at the next fork, and you will soon be following a still narrower country road. Just past a farm on your left, as the road S-bends to the right, you will take another left fork and continue on to the Information Board.
Fork right at the Information Board to pass immediately in front of the imposing **Caserio Oyarbide** with its emblazoned front elevation, and take the road down into the valley.
From just past the Caserio, you will see away below you two white houses (which you will pass) and a light brown one to their right. Make your way down (past a fountain) to this brown one, which is emblazoned "N. Barrena", and take the earth path to the left immediately opposite its flank wall. Where it forks up to the left into a field, follow it down to the right ignoring any ribbon or other livestock barrier. Only 15m or so further on is another narrower path, which goes off to the left. Follow this down to a stream, cross over the "bridge" and climb up along a rough track of stone slabs. This becomes a wider cement track before swinging left to pass between the houses **Antia** (right) and **Albitsu** (left).
Almost immediately after, you will see above your left shoulder, the 13th century **Ermita de Gurutzeta** dedicated to Nuestra Señora and containing a wooden statue purported to represent a young St James in pilgrim garb.
You now go up left to the Ermita and subsequently follow that road past a chicken battery farm. Just beyond it, turn right and go down past the cemetery, to a T-junction in Idiazabal. Here, the waymarked route goes off to the left and avoids the town centre.
Turn right if you want to visit the Church and/or take advantage of the town's facilities.

Idiazabal.   **3.7 km**
Shops, Bars, Restaurants, Chemist, Health Centre, Accommodation.
St Michael's Church with 13th century Romano-Gothic door, around which, the
church was rebuilt in C17th. The retable is 18th century.
The home of Idiazabal cheese.

If you go into the town centre, you will find, opposite the west door of the
Church, an Information Board. This will help you visualise your way ahead.
From the Information Board, go south along the old N-1 for about 300m, to a
minor crossroads with a wooden fingerpost pointing right to **Lobioko
Begiratokia** (a viewpoint). Here, you rejoin the waymarked route by turning
right to follow the finger. Proceed up and under the new N-1 to the viewpoint
and its bench seats, close to a fork in the road. From here, the waymarks will
lead you straight on and over the ridge, and then down to the GI-2637, where
you go left along a pedestrian/cyclist way, straight on at the next roundabout and
past the Ermita de la Santa Cruz into old **Segura.**

2) The Direct Road Route from Beasain to Segura.

Having entered Beasain along Kale Nagusia and gone as far as the Police
Station in the Market Hall arcade, which is on your right under a bandstand,
carry straight on to the railway station. Continuing forward, you pass a 15th
century Manor House / Museum (Palacio de Igartza), which is on the other side
of the river on your left. Going straight on at all junctions, you go under a high
viaduct and again straight on past the **Hotel Castillo** in **Iurre**.
Shortly after this, you pass some factories / workshops on your left and see a
road ahead of you, ramping upwards and going left across the N-1. This is your
route. Cross the bridge and take the 2nd turning on the right leading to a service
road fronting a commercial centre, with Carrefour and Lidl supermarkets.
By following this parallel to the N-1 to its end, you will come to a roundabout
feeding the N-1 and see a road going off to Idiazabal. This you follow for about
500m, until you reach another roundabout, (small bar on far side) where you
take the GI-2637 tourist route to Segura, with its dedicated walk/cycleway. You
will pass the Ermita of the Holy Cross as it enters

Segura   (from Idiazabal) **3.75 km**
                                             (by road from Beasain) **7.4 km**
Shops, Café / Bars, Tourist Office in Town Hall with very helpful staff and
sello, Accommodation.

This interesting walled town was founded in 1256 on the orders of Alphonso X,
King of Castile, as part of his defensive strategy.

The 14th/16th century Church of the Assumption (with bas-relief of Santiago Matamoros), the three Palaces (one of which is the present Town Hall), and the streets of the old town are now jointly designated as a National Monument to ensure the preservation of the town's medieval charm.

Continue up the main street, past the Plaza and follow the GI-2637 to

Zegama.

Alternative route to Cegama for walkers who would prefer to take a slightly longer, but far more energetic and scenic route to avoid 4.15 kms of busy road. Please note, however;
*   *There is no waymarking on this route*
*   *This route is off the beaten track. It should be quite safe to do it singly, but is would be safer to travel in at least pairs for personal physical security reasons.*

At the top of the town, there is a fork with the road to the right signed to Zegama and that to the left to Laiotza. Take the left fork; swing right opposite the Information Office and then swing left to pass in front of the Franciscan Friary on your right. Carry on along the road and take the next fork to the right, which is signed to the 'Futbol Zelaia'. Follow it past the Football Ground to where the road veers right and a narrower asphalted road goes more or less straight on. Follow this narrower road to where there are three ways ahead of you. Left and right are private, and the centre one is an earth track. Follow this steeply up past a house on your left, and straight on past another further up on your right. This second house is Caserio Pagamuño, one of the last remaining complete examples of a traditionally built house in the area.
Ultimately, the track you are on leads to the Ermita de Santa Barbara but you will leave it to drop down into Kortaberria.
Carry on up the hill ignoring all minor side turnings until you sense that you are about to climb out of the woodland you are in. When the top cover begins to clear, you will come to a T-junction where the main track goes sharply left and a slightly narrower, but very well defined rutted track bears off due west downhill to the right with conifer plantation on its right.
This is where you turn right for Kortaberria. After following the track down for about 110m, you will pass under some overhead HT lines. 50 metres later, the track will swing hard left to contour the hillside down and around until, eventually, after going right at the only fork you meet, you pass two white houses (in line and 110m apart), before meeting a tarmacced road. Turn right and follow it through its hairpin bends down to the village of Kortaberria.

(Sadly, the village is too small to support any refreshment or other facilities). When you reach the first houses on the left, turn immediately left and up into the small square serving the group of houses. Keeping straight on, exit the square towards the fields and, a few metres on, find and follow a grassy track leading off to the right along a fence. This track will lead you up to, and will swing to the right along the northern edge of woodland before turning left to start its ascent through the woods.

The track up will zigzag once (or possibly twice) before you come to a point where it swings hard left, but where a secondary distinct track angles off only slightly right and more steeply upwards. Take this secondary track. The steep section is only about 40m in length and ultimately swings left to join a much wider track at the top.

Turn right and follow it downhill past a derelict building on your right. After a couple of sharp bends, you will come to a house and the concrete lane which serves it. Carry on down the lane to reach a T-junction where you face the house 'Elorriñe'. Turn left and follow the road to its junction with the GI-2637. Turn left again and proceed with care as you walk the next 1.25 km into

Zegama (Cegama (C)).

(via alternative)	**7.9 km**
(via GI-2637)	**5.4 km**

Shops, Bars, Restaurants, Town Hall for sello, Accommodation, Chemist.

Zegama is situated in the Goerri region of Gipuzkoa Province. Philip III declared it a town in 1615, but the French subsequently destroyed it in the Wars of Independence.

The 15th / 16th century Parish Church of St. Martin contains the mausoleum of General Carlista Tomas Zumalakárregi, and the 14th century Cross of the Ermita de Santa Cruz del Monte Aizkorri, which is thought to be the oldest cross in Gipuzkoa.

• Here again, walkers are recommended to be in at least pairs for this next section of the Way.

• There are about 8.5kms of almost continuous climb from Zegama to the top of the pass, and an altitude difference of 800m. The severity of the climb is only marginally less than that of the mountain route out of St Jean Pied de Port

• The mountain pass ahead of you can be enshrouded in cloud. If you see it like this, you would be well advised to consider delaying your departure, or of investigating the logistics of an alternative route via the Puerto de Otzaurte. This is 6.5km further up the road after the turn-off for Iruetxeta, and approx. 5.5km from St Adrian's Tunnel via a well-marked and less arduous track.

• Would a taxi to the bar / restaurant at the Puerto be out of the question?

From the church, continue south along the GI-2637 road for about 1.5km and you will come to the right turn for the Apeadero de Zegama (railway halt). About 300m after this, you will see a narrow, concrete surfaced lane slanting up to the right, much adorned with yellow and other arrows, and signposted to **Iruetxeta**. Follow this lane, turning hard left at the next T-junction, and it will take you up through Iruetxeta, and past the Ermita de la Virgen de las Nieves. Do not be surprised to see the Ermita used for sundry other purposes of the adjoining caserio. Shortly after crossing the line of the railway tunnel, the lane reaches the caserio **Buenavista.** Here, the hard surface finishes. Your route turns left in front of the caserio, and then right immediately after it and up a hedge-lined earth track along the southeast edge of woodland.

After crossing a culverted watercourse, the track leads to an open area of scrub, where it continues over to the left up another track, which was (is it still?) obstructed by a fence / barrier a few metres further up. If necessary, negotiate this barrier and continue onwards and upwards through trees and bushes, until you pass between two stone pastoral huts, close on left and right hand. **Caution is needed here,** for the obvious track goes off to the left. Do not follow it. On top of the bank in front of you is another track which you follow to the right. It snakes in an elongated S-bend over heath and through woodland, until it reaches a plateau where there is situated on your right, a long, low pantiled building with stuccoed walls and green painted shutters. You are also met by a track which comes to meet you from the opposite direction, and which turns to go to your left. At this point, before taking the said track to the left, it is worth taking a few steps along the track straight ahead of you, to enjoy the view of Zegama in the valley out of which you have just climbed. Your route will lead you yet higher through scrub and woodland to the

Ermita de Santi Espiritu.   **7.0 km**
A former *ermita-hospital* run by the Templars.

From the fence immediately ahead of you, you can see in the dip to your left, a **cafe/bar/albergue**, which provides a 'sello' and accommodation (but ring first if you require accommodation). The building itself was originally a Police Station of the Mikaletes, the Gipuzkoan Provincial Police.
There is no water supply point between here and Zalduondo, so, if necessary, you can 'top up' at the bar.
As you cross the fence line, ignore any yellow arrows going to the right along the fence and proceed straight ahead along the clear path to

St Adrian's Tunnel.   **0.5 km**
The Tunnel is actually a large cave hollowed out of the hillside by the action of meltwater drainage in the dim and very distant past. From time to time in its

history, it appears to have been used as a defensively fortified place of retreat. The remains of a more recent defensive wall, with a 4m high archway for mounted horsemen, can still be seen. Behind this rampart, and within the mouth of the cave itself, is the Ermita de San Adrián.

Enter the cave, and go through the tunnel. Once through, you will find yourself walking along the remains of an original Roman *calzada*. Follow it as it climbs to the top of the pass 1km further on. Here, you will be standing under an electricity pylon on the boundary line between Gipuzkoa and Álava, and your way ahead well indicated by the Amigos de los Caminos de Santiago de Álava.
You will also see other footpaths, which follow the Aizkorri Ridge. Do not be tempted to follow them. You can always come back to do that.
At first, the path winds down through some rocks before descending steeply to a more obvious track, where you are guided left by a waymarker. After leaving this wider track for a narrower one on its right, you find yourself walking down the right hand side of a defile along a trail, which can be a bit muddy in the places where the occasional small stream crosses it. This trail leads down to a well-maintained forest road, which comes down from the right. Turn left and follow it as it zigzags down to the tarmacced road at

Zumarraundi (Zamarraundi (B)).   **3.0 km**

The tarmacked road was constructed to serve an oil drilling station, which once existed here. The site is now a large car park with compacted earth surface for the benefit of ramblers, picnickers, etc., but has no facilities.

Your route follows the road down to Zalduondo. In the process, it joins the Araya to Zalduondo road (where you turn right), passes through some open ground before going over a cattle grid and a crossroads (where you continue straight ahead), passes the turning you would take if you wanted to visit the Ermita de San Julian y Santa Basilisa (0.5km off route) and passes (on your right) a chapel and calvary.

Zalduondo (Zalduendo (C)).   **5.2 km**
Bar / Restaurant / Fountains.

Parish Church of San Saturnino (15th century), with baroque altarpiece depicting the life and martyrdom of the saint, and a carving of Santiago in pilgrim's robe.
Palace of Lazárraga, which has a 16th century plateresque door with ionic columns. The front elevation is emblazoned with a carved shield with flanking statues. It now houses a museum, with a section on the Camino de Santiago.

Passing a Camino Information board erected by the Amigos de los Caminos de Santiago de Álava, go over the staggered crossroads and leave the village by the road heading in a SW direction.

At the exit to the village, the now by-passed medieval bridge of Zubizabal can be seen on the left, as can the cross, erected by the Lazárraga family, which marks the village boundary.

The road climbs over a long low ridge and later passes near the Ermita de San Millán, standing on a rise to the right of the road as it swings left for

Ordoñana.   **3.0 km**
An old house, on the right as you enter the village, has a carved shield and inscription. Parish Church of the Assumption.

Carry on through the village and follow the road past the church and the sports centre. It will bend to the right and then left as it passes the communal weighbridge. It will shortly be joined from the right by the road from Luzuriaga. Another kilometre brings you to a road on your left, which goes to Mezquia, and, a few metres beyond that, is a private house, the former Hospital of San Lázaro y la Magdalena, which still carries on its façade, the shield of Salvatierra, the inscription "S. MAR. MAGDALENA" and a relief of a vessel, which alludes to the one, filled with perfume, given to Jesus by the Saint.

Further on still, on the right behind a hedge, you might be able to spot the Cross of Ventaberri, whose spirally grooved column is surmounted by the figure of a weeping Mary at the foot of the cross.

Shortly after this you reach a roundabout on the north edge of the old town of

Salvatierra (Agurain (B)).   **3.0 km**
Shops, Bar / Restaurants, Post Office, Accommodation, Tourist / Camino Information Office for sello, Chemist
The Fiesta de Nuestra Señora del Rosario, involving a large bonfire in the Plaza de San Juan, takes place on 15 August with, of course, much merrymaking.

If you wish to see the wall paintings in the Church of St Martin in Gaceo (the next village), or those in the Church of Alaiza which are equally notable (see later), you are advised to contact the priest of St John's Church or enquire at the Tourist Office for information regarding the possibility of access. During school holidays, there may be prearranged opening times for both churches.

To avoid the tolls which were charged in days of old, many pilgrims used to branch off to the right to follow the outside of the town's west walls.

To go through the town, follow the arrows over the roundabout and up the road to the left of the Church of Santa Maria. Cross over the road to join the walkway along the north wall of the Church, and then turn left in front of the Church and into the **Calle Mayor**, in which you will find numerous bars, a hostal/restaurant and some shops. At its far end is the main square, the Church of St John and an Information Office (open mid June to September).

Opposite the Church is an arcade supported by medieval pillars known as "Las olbeas" and under which markets are held.

From the square, continue south via **Portal del Rey**, turn right along the old main road (**Calle Fueros**) and continue past the waste disposal site, opposite which the alternative route emerges near the remains of the Cross of Arnicrúz. Shortly after, you will come to a major junction with the *autopista* approach road. Keep straight ahead and follow the service road, fronting a large factory.

Continue along the service road in front of the cement works (Agurain Hormigones Mac S.A), and, just after the works, move onto the main road verge on your right. Continue along this verge until you come to a service road, (opposite a Same Tractors (?) outlet), which feeds the industrial estate. Turn left down this access road and then go right at the next roundabout along the main estate road. After about 650m or so, another road turns off left, and leads to the bridge/tunnel under the *autopista* through which the Way passes. At this bridge, the tarmacked road reverts to a compacted gravel agricultural road and leads you to

Gazeo (Gaceo (C)).   3.9 km
Fountain by weighbridge.
Romanesque Church of San Martín (13th century) with beautiful wallpaintings.

Once past the church, turn left along the road to Alaiza. After 350 m, and before you reach the railway, your route is waymarked to the right.

*If you have arranged to visit Alaiza Church, instead of turning right at this point, continue for 3km straight ahead over the railway bridge. You will pass through **Langarica** and reach a T-junction. Here, a right turn followed by an immediate left turn will bring you into **Alaiza** at the end of another 500m.*
The church is famous for the Gothic murals in its apse and sacristy, which depict wildlife scenes and scenes from battles and daily life. They also include the group of pilgrims which has become so well known by having been reproduced so many times in literature about the Camino.

If you take this diversion it will be necessary to return as far as Langarica and then branch left, making directly for Ezquerecocha.

If you do not want to go to Alaiza, turn right to take the narrow asphalt road through the fields to

Ezkerekotxa (Ezquerecocha (C)).   **2.0 km**
Parish Church of San Román with 12th century portico. The octagonal apse has an interesting early Gothic window. There is also a statue of San Martín Laborador, and a bust of San Román with juvenile representations of San Rocco and San Sebastián on either side of him.

Continue past the church to the central crossroads and turn left to go to the railway station. As you approach the railway, do not take the track over it, but turn right and follow the road parallel to it, with the station on your left. The route now takes you up and round the Alto de Chinchetru, through which the railway is tunnelled. However, when the road swings left over the tunnel, your route lies straight ahead along a gravel agricultural road (still parallel to the railway on your left). The track gradually drops until you reach the supports of a new bridge, which has replaced a level crossing. Here, you must turn right and continue forward, i.e. northwards, for about 200m (without crossing the bridge) before veering left in a roughly westerly direction to follow the *Camino de los Romanos*. This you follow without deviation to the next main road you reach.
Turn right at the T-junction in the agricultural road to access the main road, and then walk about 100m left towards Alegria. You have now reached a

Turn off point for Alegria-Dulantzi (C-B)   *4.50 km*

The town lies 1.75km in front of you. There you can find accommodation, shops and bars and visit the Church of San Blas, which has romanesque elements. You can rejoin the Camino by walking 1.15 km out of Alegria to the Ermita de Nuestra Señora de Ayala (see below)

If you have decided not to go into Alegria from this point, turn right and follow the agricultural road until you reach a local road, which leads (left) to Alegria and (right) to the immediately adjoining access road to the

Ermita de Nuestra Señora de Ayala.   **1.5 km**
Formerly, it was the parish church of the area before the latter became depopulated. It is a beautiful building of 13th century construction with a barrel-vaulted nave of three spans, and a semicircular apse with carved consoles, one of which bears scallop shells. It has an unusual portico with four arches, three pointed and one rounded. To its rear is a picnic area with fountain.

28

From the Ermita return to the agricultural road along which you have just come, go 10m past it, and, if you have decided not to access Alegria from this point, turn right along another agricultural road to continue along the *Camino de los Romanos* and then bridge a stream to reach the **Ermita of San Juan de Arrarain.** (Built in the 12th century, it has a semicircular apse and vaulted ceiling. Some of the columns are decorated with scallop shells. At one time it provided shelter for pilgrims). Continuing on, you cross the railway line, the River Alegria and the Vitoria road, to arrive at a *lavadero* at the entrance to

Elburgo (Burgelu(B)).   **2.8 km**
No facilities, apart from a fountain, which is understood now to be connected to mains water. (The villagers drink the water despite an old "not drinkable" sign.)

Pass the pillar surmounted by an iron cross, and arrive at the 15th / 16th century Parish Church of San Pedro, which has a gothic font, a baroque altarpiece with a statue of Santiago, and, outside, a neo-classical tower.
Go past the buildings on the south side of the church along the agricultural road, which first of all crosses a stream and then comes to a fork. Take the right fork, and after a while, you will reach a bollarded intersection which is the

Turn off point for Santuario de Estíbaliz   *1.6 km*

At this intersection, you can turn right to follow the gravel walkway along the bed of the former rail link between Villafranca (away on your left) and Estíbaliz (out of sight on a hill ahead and to your right) You will pass through a cutting and then, at another signposted junction of walkways, turn right to reach

Santuario de Ntra Señora de Estíbaliz.   *1.3 km*
Café / bar and visitor centre. Limited pilgrim accommodation.

Founded in 932 it was both a fortress and a monastery, which came under the rule of the monastery of Santa Maria la Real de Nájera.
The existing building is of Transitional Romanesque style, and was built on the site of a former building of the 11th century. It is of latin cross plan, with three semicircular apses and a two arched tower over the door known as the "Speciosa". The doorway itself has four decorated archivolts.
The sanctuary is administered by the Order of San Benito, which holds daily services and is able to offer a limited amount of guest accommodation to pilgrims.

After visiting the sanctuary it is possible to rejoin the Camino:-
EITHER by retracing your steps to the above-mentioned signposted junction of

29

*walkways, and continuing straight over it to follow the pathway down to the church in **Villafranca (1.1km)**, where you will find the Camino signposted to the right,*
*OR by taking the walkway alongside the road to **Argandoña (1.75 km)***

If you are not visiting the sanctuary go straight ahead, across the bollarded crossway, and along the agricultural road, down into

Villafranca.   **1.1 km**
The Parish Church of San Andrés has an interesting plateresque doorway, and a scallop shell, carved in a recess, to indicate the church's connection with the Way of St James.
From the church, take the signposted track across the fields to

Argandoña.   **1.3 km**
13th century Parish Church of Santa Columba, with semi-circular apse and a pointed arched doorway with four decorated columns.

Your route through the village brings you to the road, which comes down from your right from Estíbaliz. Turn left along it, and follow it round to the right. A few metres further on, you will turn into the road going north to Zerio, and then go immediately left to follow a section of abandoned road. This abandoned road parallels the nearby N-130/A-132 (the Estella to Vitoria road) for about 500m before you join it to walk the remaining 2.0km to the junction at

Askartza (Ascarza (C)).   **2.7 km**
From here, turn left towards Otazu, and pass the road leading to the cemetery of San Salvadór. About 650m along the road look for a right turn onto an agricultural road, and follow this to the T-junction at its end. Turn left and walk the remaining 300m into

Arcaya.   **2.0 km**
Picnic area with Fountain. Private Refuge (Casa de la Spiritualidad, Leku).
As the village is approached, a left turn down the road to Otazu, near the village weighbridge, will bring you to the remains of some Roman baths.
The existing Parish Church of the Natividad de Nuestra Señora is an enlargement of an older church but retains many romanesque elements as well as a great baroque altarpiece and the original tower.
Twin towered *Palacio* of the Barons of Arcaya.

After passing in front of the Church and swinging left round the picnic area, you fork right before crossing the Río Santo Tomás. Continue straight ahead to the top of a low ridge. At its crest, the way ahead is currently blocked, but by diverting up into the field on the right, you will see not only the large-scale development works necessitating the block, but also a distinct earth path down the slope to a new single carriageway about 50m ahead of you and a new dual carriageway about 175m beyond that.

I believe it is proposed, as part of the scheme of redevelopment, to provide a walk/cycleway down to and across the dual carriageway to link up with a paseo going to right and left through a proposed green area along the Errekaleor Stream. This would certainly be of benefit pilgrims but, for the meantime, make your way down to the

Dual Carriageway   **1.1 km**

At this point, you have a **choice**. You can take **EITHER** a route via **Vitoria city centre OR** a route through the **southern outskirts.** Neither route is currently waymarked, but the following route descriptions and the plans on pages 32 and 33 (post) should help you navigate them.

To get to the Refuge, follow the 'outskirts' route as far as the entrance to the Parkway. Look for Paseo de la Zumaquera. It is just to your right leading off a small roundabout in the road immediately adjoining the parkway. Follow it to and along its continuation (Calle de Álava). On the right, before a river bridge where the road continues as Calle de Salvatierrabide, is Calle de Isaac Diaz.

1) The Route via the outskirts.
In the absence of the proposed walk/cycle way, turn left along the dual carriageway and follow it, over the Errekaleor Stream, to what can only be described as the end of a very large elongated roundabout. Going straight ahead, over the end of the roundabout, you will see and follow **Calle Venta de la Estrella** up to and around a small roundabout. Continue along Calle Venta d/l Estrella by means of the footpath on its left to another larger and more complicated roundabout. Here, you will find yourself under a pylon.

Straight ahead of you, you will see a continuous set of three zebra crossings and you will notice a cycle facility incorporated with them. Follow the crossings and you will see the cycleway and a pedestrian walkway entering a wooded **Parkway**.

This is the start of a Paseo, with shops and bars situated one or two streets over to the right of it. By following the Paseo and by keeping straight ahead at all junctions and crossings you will ultimately reach the Avenida San Prudencio immediately below a crossroad, where, going left is **Calle Uleta**.

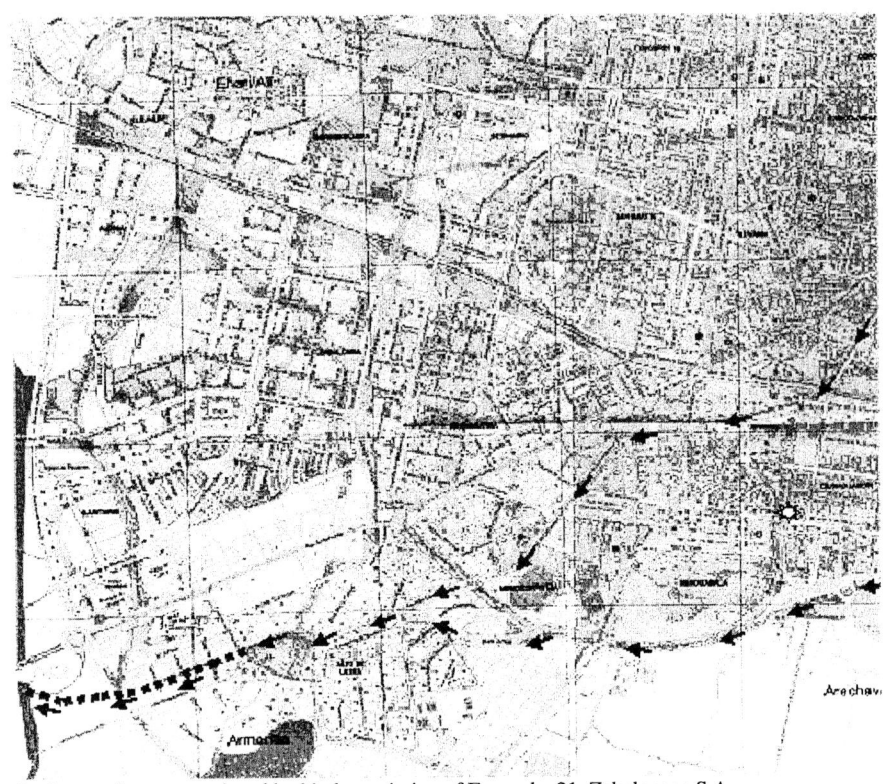

Background map reproduced by kind permission of Ensanche 21, Zabalgunea S.A.

◀— ◀— ◀—   Described routes
■ ■ ■ ■ ■ ■ ■ ■   [Proposed walk/cycleway after Arcaya
[New walk/cycleway in Armentia.
✿   Albergue Juvenil Carlos Abaitua, Calle Isaac Diaz.

2) The City Centre Route

In the absence of the proposed walk/cycleway, turn right along the dual carriageway and, at the first roundabout, turn left. Cross the bridge over the Errekaleor Stream and walk on to another dual carriageway. Cross over it and take the road directly ahead of you (**Itinerario de Antonino**) in front of the high-rise blocks. At the end of this road, follow the pathway up through the greenway and then go right to reach the railway line and use the footbridge you can see crossing it. Once you have reached the other side of the railway, turn left along **La Florida** and continue along it, over a set of traffic lights near the new bullring (El Correo to the left), until you reach, 200m further on, a small square. Leave this square via the far right hand corner along **Calle Angulema** to reach

32

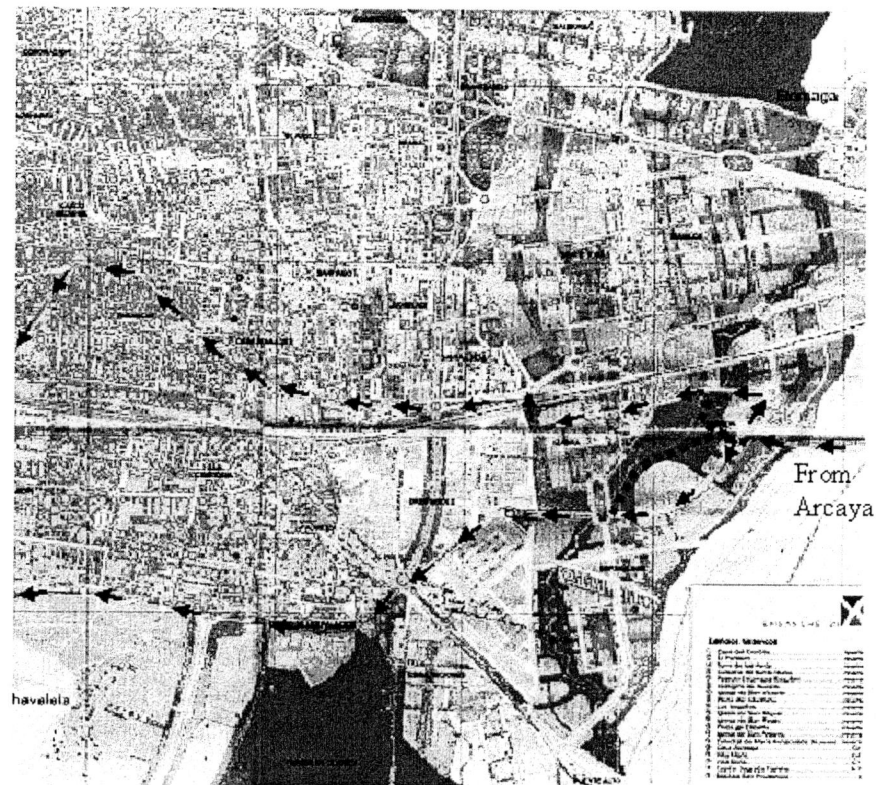

From Arcaya

havalala

Background map reproduced by kind permission of Ensanche 21, Zabalgunea S.A.

the **Plaza de Nuestra Señora de los Desamparados.** Cross the square diagonally to find **Calle de la Independencia,** which will bring you to the main Post Office not far from the **Plaza de España** in the centre of

Vitoria-Gasteiz (C-B). (To Plaza de España) **2.9 km**

From the Plaza de España you can easily access the Old City. (See map on P.34.)

In its early days, **Vitoria** was a strategically based village on a Roman trade route. It was granted a Fuero (Charter) by King Sancho VI (the Wise) in 1181, and was captured by Alfonso VIII in 1200. Alfonso X granted it a Royal Charter in 1271 and Juan II elevated it to city status.

It is the principal town of the province of Álava (Áraba(C)) and also the seat of administration of the whole of the Basque Autonomous Region (Álava, Viscaya, Guipuzcoa and parts of Navarra). This is in spite of the fact that there are fewer speakers of the Basque language in Álava than in the other regions.

(continued on P 36)

The Old City, Vitoria-Gasteiz

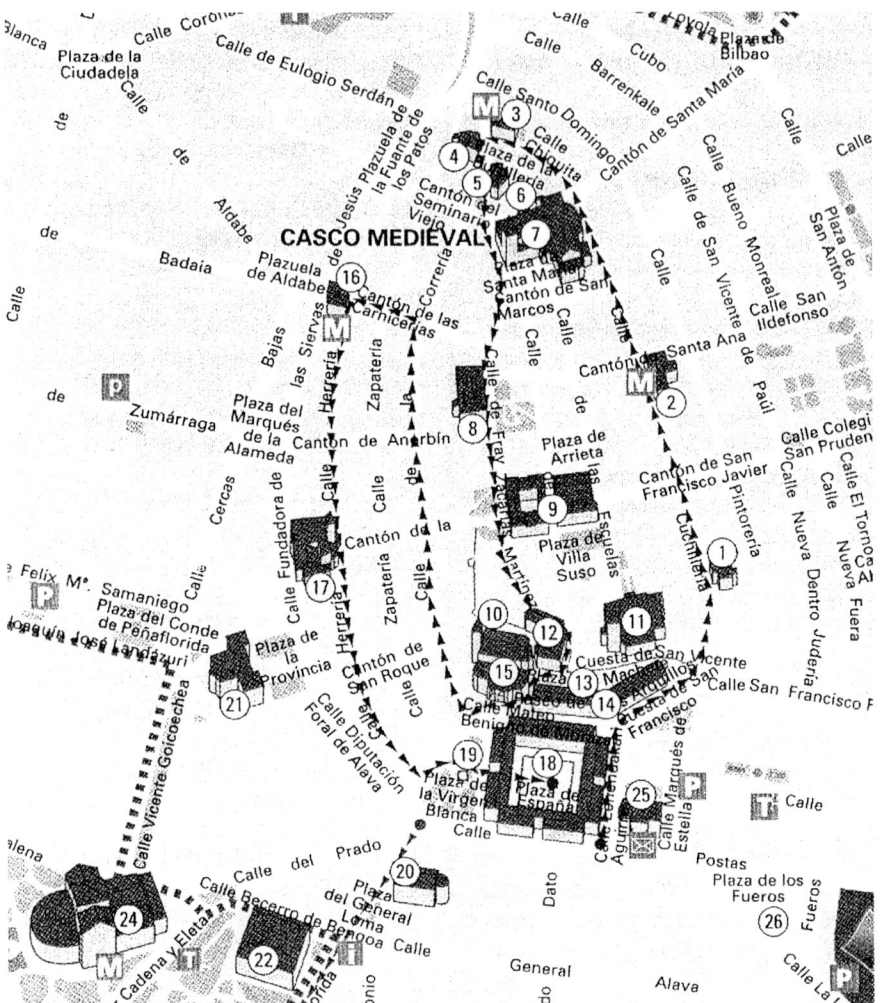

Reproduced and amended by kind permission of Gobierno Vasco, Departmento de Comercio, Consumo y Turismo. ©

The Old City, Vitoria - Gasteiz

Index to Street Plan: -

1 Casa Del Cordón –   15th C. Has a medieval tower and a gothic hall.

2 Palacio de Bendaña –   1525. Houses the Fournier Playing Card Museum

3 Casa Armero d/los Gobeo – Late 16th C. Home of the Gobeo family. Now houses the Archeological Museum.

4 El Portalón –   Late 15th C. Originally a stagecoach inn. Now a restaurant.

5 Tower of the Anda fam. –   15th C fortified house.

6 Plaza de la Brulleria –   A 1985 square with traditional skittles piste.

7 Cathedral of St Mary –   14th C. Triple gothic portico and v. high nave.

8 Pal. de Escoriaza-Esquivel – 1540. Renaissance pal with plateresque door.

9 Palacio de Montehermoso – 1524. Now the Montehermoso cultural centre.

10 Remains of Old City walls – 12th C.

11 Church of San Vicente –   15th C. Example of Basque-gothic style.

12 Palacio de Villa Suso –   16th C. Built on the original town walls. Now a Conference Centre.

13 Plaza del Machete –   A place where oaths were taken over a machete.

14 Los Arquillos –   Late 18th C. Gp of small squares surrounded by houses of interesting architecture.

15 Church of San Miguel –   14th C

16 Tower de Doña Otxanda –   1970 tower built on remains of a 15th C house.

17 Church of San Pedro –   14th C. Four religious scenes in tympanum and image of the Virgin in the mullion.

18 Plaza de España –   1791. A perfect square housing the main offices of the Town Hall on one of its sides.

19 Plaza de la Virgen Blanca.   Battle of Vitoria Monument at its centre.

20 Church of St Anthony.

21 Palacio de la Provincia.

22 Basque Parliament Buildings.

24 New Cathedral of St Mary.

25 Post Office.

The Tourist Information Office is situated in Plaza de General Loma at the SW corner of Plaza de la Virgen Blanca. The Office is at the junction of Paseo de la Florida and C/ San Antonio (**i** next to building No22 on the map).
Sellos are obtainable there, and from the Old Cathedral of St Mary where tours of its current restoration works are organised.

Exit the City by following the waymarks. Leave the **Plaza de la Virgen Blanca** via the **Plaza de General Loma** and, passing the Tourism Office on your left, go down the **Paseo de la Florida**. This becomes the **Paseo de la Senda** before passing under the railway. Immediately after the railway bridge, fork right along the **Paseo Fray Francisco de Vitoria** passing the **Museo de Armeria** and keep straight on to go past the **Parque del Prado**, which is on your right. When the **Capilla de la Sagrada Familia** is reached, the avenue bends to the left and becomes the **Paseo de Cervantes**. Follow this past the **Sports Stadium** on your left and eventually veer right into the **Avenida San Prudencio,** About 250m after passing over a bridge over a road below you, you will link up with the route through the outskirts, which joins you from your left, just before

Calle Uleta	(From Pl de España)	**2.5 km**
	(From dual carriageway)	**4.6 km**

Continue up **Avenida de San Prudencio** to the top of the rise, where there is a multi-crossroads with a monument to, and statue of San Prudencio. (A cider bar is only a little way up the 1st exit on the left). From the monument you continue straight on along the Avenida, taking in the view of the imposing 12th century (with 17th century rebuilding) **Basilica of San Prudencio** on the outskirts of

Armentia.   **0.5 km**
Accommodation (expensive). Bar. Shops?

San Prudencio, the Patron Saint of Álava, is a famous son of Armentia.
It was originally a Roman town and later, in the 11th century, became the seat of the Archbishopric of Calahorra, which moved there when that area was threatened by the Moors.

Continue to the crossroads at the top of Avenida de San Prudencio. Ahead of you is the new Paseo del Peregrino, which you follow to its end and go straight over a roundabout. Go straight over the next cross roads (left for Eskibel – right for Dog Refuge) and pass a shooting range on your left. You will next pass an access roundabout to the N-102 before reaching a pilgrim friendly bar at a now disused service station opposite **Camping Ibaia**. 1Km further on finds you in.

Gomecha (Gometxa (B)).   **2.75km**
No facilities.
Parish Church of the Transfiguration. Some consoles and the base of the font
remain from the medieval building.
There used to be a hermitage dedicated to Santiago.

Turn right by the church along a track which heads SW. After about 2.4km, you
will come to the road from Ariñez (situated away to your right on the N-1).
Cross this secondary road and continue along the track to arrive at a non-
chlorinated water trough on the eastern edge of

Subijana (Subillana (C)) de Álava.   **4.5km**
Picnic area and fountain opposite the church. If you want to use the Hotel Ruta
de Europa, it is situated 1.7km down the road to the new A-1.

Parish Church of San Estéban (16th century), with detached bell tower.
Simón de Anda, who earned his fame in Spanish history by defeating the
English fleet in the Philippines before becoming Captain General of the Islands,
was born in the Casa-Palacio, in 1710.

In the past, two routes out of Subijana were waymarked. Now, only the hill
route is marked, partly because the construction of Autovia A-1 has resulted in
the closure of a length of the former N-1. However, a route exists along the
valley by which walkers can get to La Puebla, when they consider the ground or
weather conditions are too bad for them. Since the hill route is impassable by
cyclists, I will describe them both.

The valley route.
From the water trough, turn right and go down the hill towards the church.
Turn left at the end of the wedge-shaped play/picnic area to pass to the right of
the church. Ignore the road to the left behind the church and go straight ahead
along an agricultural road, ignoring the track which leads off to the right.
Follow the track without deviation all the way down to the motorway, and turn
left along the agricultural road which parallels it. Continue along this track
past one bridge over the A-1 to the second bridge over it. Cross the motorway
by this second bridge and you will find the access to the now little used length
of the N-1 alongside the start of the A-1 (South) access road. Your route has a
compacted earth surface and, at first, drops down towards the A-1 before
veering right to meet the tarmacced surface of the N-1 about 400m further on.
This will take you to the roundabout where the hill route from Villanueva de la
Oca emerges. Turn right to take the old road into La Puebla de Arganzón.

The hill route.
From the water trough where you entered the village, take the lane to the left of the low wall straight ahead of you, and follow the lane up and left past the *Casa-Palacio*. Carry on to a more open scrubby area, where there are vestiges of an old fence to right and left of you. Here you turn right to follow a well defined track, which continues gradually up and around the hillside, through an opening in a wire boundary fence, past the site of a new prison (on your right) and through woodland before reaching a crossroads in the footpath system Tracks go right and left, but you continue straight ahead into what appears to be a small glade.

You are now in an area, which was formerly a restricted military zone. Your path will immediately swing left out of the glade to follow a path through scrubby woodland, before climbing to the highest point of this section (c.760m). Here, the route is joined by a track descending from the ridge up on your left. Shortly, you will pass through a clearing in the scrub, and, not long after, you will follow the very steep, and loose stony track, which descends to the SW, and then S, before reaching some cultivated fields and a concrete bridge over a stream. The waymarker here is a bit ambiguous but you can either cross the bridge to follow the more pleasant path alongside the stream, or continue along the track you are on until you enter

Villanueva de la Oca.   **5.0km**
No facilities apart from some seats by the fountain as you enter the village, where you might rest and refill your water bottles.
The Parish Church of San Pedro and its large tower stand on a small hill.

From the seats, walk up to the road junction in front of the church and turn right. This road will eventually lead you under the motorway to a roundabout on a now very little used N-1. Go round the roundabout to reach the minor road straight ahead which will take you into

La Puebla de Arganzón.   **3.3 km**
(Valley route from Subijana)   **9.00 km**
Bars, Shops, Restaurants, Accommodation, Bus stop and Railway Station.
Ring Town Hall 1 or 2 days in advance (between 0900 and 1400) if you want to use the Casa del Peregrino. Collect sello and keys for C del P from TH.
It was a walled town in the middle ages. The Parish Church of the Assumption in C/de Santiago was originally fortified and has a gothic entrance.
The old bridge over the Arganzón is worth seeing.
Near the exit of the town is the Ermita de Nuestra Señora de la Antigua with massive columns in the apse and a pointed arched tower. The former Hospital of San Juan Evangelista forms part of the same building.

From the parish church, go south past the sports hall, past the Ermita de Nuestra Señora to the next crossroad, where there is a bus stop on the near left corner. Here you will turn left and go up over the railway. While at the upper level, you will see slip roads left and right, up from and down to the now little used southbound carriageway of the N-1. Take the right hand slip road, which is signposted to Burgueta, and follow the N-1 south for approx 1.5kms. The marked Way will then take you left towards Pangua, San Formerío and San Estéban and under the motorway. Immediately after the motorway, you will turn right and walk parallel to it for 1.0km before reaching a T-junction. There is a service station and bar/restaurant to the right via a bridge under the motorway, but your way is marked to the left. This road will lead you eastwards to

Burgueta.   **4.2 km**
Sello available in the Community Centre opposite the Church
Fountain and water trough near the swimming pool, where, reportedly, you can find a telephone.
Parish Church of San Martín, (altered over the years), with 13th century portico, a tower with three arched openings and a cobbled icthys in front of the portico.

On entering the village, follow the hairpin road round to the left to access the church and the main square with the water troughs at a crossroads. Turn right at this crossroads to take the road going SW. This will lead you down to the new residential area (San Andrés), where you will go straight across a crossroads. If there has been no further development in the interim, the metalled road ahead will finish abruptly after 30m or so, and revert to its original status as an agricultural road. This you will follow for about 2km until you come to a 6-way crossing. The main track going 2nd left becomes metalled and is recommended if you want to visit the bar/restaurant (open every day except Mondays) at the top of the village. The track straight ahead goes to an aircraft radio beacon. The waymarked track is the one going 3rd left downhill towards 10 o'clock. This is part of the old *"Camino de los Peregrinos,"* a now improved track, which winds down to the lower end of

Estavillo (Estanillo (C)/Estabelu (B)).   **2.2 km**
Bar/Restaurant at top of village. Parish Church of San Martín with imposing 15th century gothic doorway.

If you have visited the bar, follow the road down through the village, diverting to visit the church if you wish. At the bottom of the village, take the road to Armiñón, which leaves the village at its SW corner with the church high above your left shoulder. After 200m, the new road veers to the right, but beyond the crash barriers on the left, you can see an agricultural road, leading straight ahead parallel to the motorway, and a waymarker pointing right to **Armiñón** and **Burgos**.

Here, you have an option, You can **either** follow the **"Camino de Santiago (por la Rioja)"** (continued below) **or** turn right to follow the waymarked route to **Burgos** (continued on P44).

While the Burgos route is the shorter route to Santiago, I imagine that the Santo Domingo route was chosen by pilgrims, who wanted to avoid what could formerly have been a difficult and possibly unsafe passage through the Pancorbo Gorge.

PART I (B) - ESTAVILLO to SANTO DOMINGO d/l CALZADA

Take the route **Por La Rioja** and follow the agricultural road past the *autopista* toll complex off on your right. At the next T-junction, go right then immediately left. Now carry straight on without deviation, until this undulating route reaches the Rio Ayuda, about 3.6km further on, on the northwest outskirts of Berantevilla.
After crossing the river (not before), you can either take the track, which veers left into the centre of the village, or continue straight on to a T-junction, where you join the L-121 Treviño / Miranda road just to the west of

Berantevilla.   **5.5 km**
Bar (no food) and clinic at eastern end of the village.
A Café / bar (closed on Wednesdays), opposite Church of the Assumption, sells a limited selection of provisions.
Town Hall, for information and sello, is opposite the church in the main street.
Refuge facilities in Centro Social.

2km west, along the road to Miranda, is the Ermita of the Virgin of Lacorzanilla, erected in 1678 by Francisco de Montoya y Allende-Salazár. Close by it is the Ermita de San Antón.

From the centre of the village, take the L-121 (west) to rejoin the route, which emerges at the T-junction 150m west of the village. Continue W for a further 50m and find the road to the left, which leads to the cemetery.

If you wish to visit the above-mentioned Ermitas, continue along the L-121 to its junction with the N-124, in the vicinity of which they are located. To rejoin the Way, go south (left) along the N-124 to Zambrana, take a left fork into the village at a bus stop. Keep left through a plaza and turn left 50m after leaving it. Walk 80 m to the church, and turn right to rejoin the waymarked route.

If not visiting the Ermitas, turn left towards the cemetery and follow the track to the right of the cemetery and up the hill to its rear. Turn right up a grassy lane, which continues to climb. Ignoring any paths which come in from the left, you contour the lower slopes of the ridge and gradually descend again towards cultivated fields, which the route borders for a while. It then veers steeply up the hill to the left, before turning right to pass along the lower edge of a rectangular stand of nut/fruit trees and towards a tall electricity pylon. Turn left to walk up along the far side of the stand of trees to the ridge, where you will find a distinct track descending steeply towards

Zambrana. 3.2 km
One bar (no food) on main N-124. No accommodation. Bus stop.
Parish Church of Santa Lucia with double arched portico in the old village centre.
Sello in Church or, if closed, next door.

Entering the village, you will pass a new development with sports field on your right. Waymarks will guide you to the Church. When you reach the church on your right, continue forward to a junction near a large rectangular water trough / *abrevadero.* Here you will turn right then immediately left. Soon, the road continues as an agricultural road, which leads south from the southeast corner of the village. It crosses a secondary road before reaching the ruined *Venta de Molino,* shortly after which, it brings you out onto the N-124.
Turn left along the N-124 and follow it through a shallow defile, and past some disused quarry buildings / plant, which are near Km post 34. About 250m further on, take the track off to the left. (If you reach a petrol station with bar / restaurant facilities, you have gone about 300m too far.) The track climbs gently round to the left over the lower slopes of Monte Cabrera until it swings to the right to bring you to a *lavadero* at the end of a road on your right, which gives access to the East Gate of

Salinillas de Buradón (Buradón Gatzaga (B)). 6.25 km
Café / Bar (often closed), some Shops. Accommodation. Fountain at East Gate.
Parish Church of the Immaculate Conception (15th century) with polygonal apse and a 17th century portico and tower. Hospital of Santa Ana.
The walled town is on the site of an Iron Age fort, which was later occupied by the Romans, whose salt exploitation gave the name *Salinillas.*
Swimming pool / bar / restaurant complex (open summer season only)

Go back out of the East Gate of the town, and turn right at the *lavadero*. Follow the waymarked route (which for this stretch of the journey is coincident with the GR91) up past the cemetery on your right and into the hills. You will follow a fairly wide earth track past a number of junctions up to a col at about 700m altitude, with the main summit of La Lobera away to the left.

At the col, two separate concrete Utility sheds indicate a **dangerous descent** ahead - 100m of descent in 350m of going. Take care down the route ahead, as it is rutted and covered with loose stones. It will lead you across an east-facing slope down the right hand side of a valley, and on through vineyards. You will eventually pass through a gap in a mound-like ridge where there is a blue notice board. Beyond the gap, the track swings right under some overhead electricity wires before reaching a junction of ways. The Camino is signed to the left and the GR91 straight on. If you intend to visit **El Portal de la Rioja**, continue along the GR91 since this will shorten the overall distance to be walked. Otherwise the Camino de Santiago will take you directly to the LR-132, where you go left to find the right turn into

Briñas.   **4.75 km**
Bars. Restaurants. Shops.
Imposing Parish church of the Assumption with staircase and tower.

Accommodation can be found at El Portal de la Rioja, a pilgrim-friendly Hotel/Bar/Restaurant 0.7km along LR-132 to the west of the town (see above).

Make your way down past the church to the Rio Ebro. Turn right along the old road to Haro, running SW and parallel to the river. Follow it for about 1.6km, and turn left to cross the Ebro by the old arched, narrow Briñas Bridge, the parapets of which have been recently renovated. Turn right at its far end. Go past a memorial to those locals who fell in the Carlist Wars, and a farm. You will reach a ramp on / off the Haro / Vitoria road. Turn right down the ramp and follow the road round left past numerous *bodegas*, before turning right to pass under the railway bridge. Swing left to follow a tributary of the Ebro, and turn left over a bridge crossing it. Continue straight on up the **Calle Navarra** to the **Plaza de la Paz**, near which you will find the Church of St Thomas in

Haro.   **3.75km**
All facilities available including Pilgrim Refuge, which you can reach by going straight ahead as you enter Plaza Castañares de Rioja to access C/ Manuel Bartolome Cossio and then taking first left into Avda Juan Carlos.

From the Plaza de la Paz, take the **Calle Virgen de la Vega** and follow it round to the **Basílica de Nstra Señora de la Vega** and up **Castañares de Rioja** to the

Plaza of the same name. Out of this Square to your right, lead the Avenida Sto Domingo (to the right of the Bullring), and the **Avda San Millán** (to the left of the Bullring). It is this latter Avenue that you must take—it is the **N-203** to Zarratón (and to Santo Domingo).

Shortly, you will pass the Bodegas Paternina on your right and continue on to a bridge over a motorway. Having crossed it, turn immediately right and follow the farm road parallel to the motorway.

After about 325m, turn left to follow another track as it rises to the southwest. Eventually, having ignored all side turnings, you will reach the top of the ridge. You then pass under some HT wires and swing left (south), before crossing the Pancorbo to Haro/Logroño road (N-232). There is a pedestrian footbridge over to your right if you should need it.

The farm track continues south, and you can see Zarratón directly ahead of you. After 500m, the track turns right (west), and after a further 250m, left (south) down the stem of a T-junction, with Zarratón once again straight in front of you. Follow this track to its end, bear right and look on your left for a grassier, but rutted track in a shallow cutting. This will lead you down into the sometimes wet and muddy wash lands of the Rio Zamaca, before taking you up again to link with the road from Casalarreina, which will take you past the church into

Zarratón.   **8.5km**
Bar / Restaurant, Shop, Fountains (one is incorporated into the Memorial to Maestro Pinedo). Parish Church of Nuestra Señora de la Asunción.

Where the road from Casalarreina joins the main street (N-203 from Haro), turn right and follow it for about 170m until it veers left at an open area with a central planting plot at the southwest end of the village. Cross this open area to its far right corner, and you will find a concrete road, which rises towards the fields behind it. It will lead you to a grassy track along an embankment rising on the right.

This track, which bypasses Cidamón and San Torcuato, passes a farmhouse known as Madrid, (beware of dogs on the loose) and crosses a local road as it makes its way to rejoin the N-203 approximately 750m before

Bañares.   **6.0km**
Bar / Restaurants, Shops, Clinic, Fountain.
Two Churches of the Holy Cross (one 12th century and the other 16th century).

Go down the main street, and the yellow arrows will guide you round to the 16th century church (with its 12th century neighbour) to find a street at the side of a bar, which will take you to the southern outskirts of the town.

From here, you take a farm road, which swings to the right over two or three riverbeds before heading straight for Santo Domingo, now visible ahead of you.

Before entering the town, you cross the by-pass road and turn left along what looks like an old railway bed. You will pass a white electricity tower and the bull ring before joining the Camino Francés into

SANTO DOMINGO DE LA CALZADA.   **5.0km**

PART I (C) - ESTAVILLO TO BURGOS

I have not walked this route and can only give the bare outline set out on the web pages of Mundicamino – "A Complete Guide to Camino de Santiago": - www.mundicamino.com > Via de Bayona .

Estavillo (Estanillo (C) /Estabelu (B)).	**0.00kms**
Armiñon	**1.10kms**
No information	
Ribagude	**4.00kms**
No information	
Lacorzana	**1.60kms**
No information	
Bayas	**3.50kms**
No information	
Miranda de Ebro	**2.50kms**
All facilities.	
Refuge in Albergue Juvenil Fernán Gonzales, C/Anduva, 82. Tel:-947 320932	
Amigos del Camino de Miranda de Ebro. Tel:- 947 325835 or 696 368053	
Orón	**3.50kms**
No information	
Ameyugo	**7.90kms**
No information (but will have shop and bar etc facilities.)	
Pancorbo	**5.30kms**
No information, (but will have shop and bar etc facilities.)	
Pilgrim Refuge – Albergue Parroquial C/Real, 21. (Ask at the Church)	
Zuñedo	**11.20kms**
No information	
Grisaleña	**3.70kms**
No information	
Cameno	**4.10kms**
No information	

Briviesca   4.40kms
No information (but will have shop and bar etc facilities.)
Pensión Casa Cuevas, Avda Félix Rodriguez de la Fuente, 11.
Tel :- 947 592079
Prádanos de Bureba   6.50kms
No information
Castil de Peones   4.00kms
No information
Revillagodos   2.00kms
No information
Quintanavides   2.40kms
No information
Sta Olalla de Bureba   1.50kms
No information
Monasterio de Rodilla   3.40kms
No information (but will have shop and bar etc facilities.)
HR Picon del Conde, Tel:- 947594355
Barrio de Sta Marina   1.20kms
No information
Ermita de Ntra Sra del Valle   0.40kms
No information
Cumbre de la Brújula   2.90kms
No information
HR La Brújula, N-1. Tel:- 947 430391
Las Mijaradas   10.2kms
No information
Hurones   2.20kms
No information
Villayerno Morquillas   1.70kms
No information
Villimar   4.00kms
No information
Burgos Cathedral   5.75kms
Refer to Pilgrims' Guide No1 – "The Camino Francés"
Total Distance for this Section   **100.95kms**

PART II - THE CYCLISTS' ROUTE
(To be read in conjunction with the walkers' section)

Note

In considering the degree of difficulty facing cyclists, assumptions have been made, that the "typical cyclist pilgrim" will be fairly fit, will be riding a sturdy, well-maintained machine, which is reasonably well laden, and that the paths and tracks etc are generally dry.

Routes alternative to the walking routes are suggested below, where it is thought that the "typical cyclist pilgrim" cannot reasonably manage the walkers' route.

That being said, the author does not guarantee that, where no alternative route is suggested, the walkers' route will be passable on two wheels.

Neither does he guarantee that the alternative route will be passable at all times and by all pilgrims. It must be left to the individual to plan and decide his / her own route as fitness, load, weather and any other circumstances dictate.

PART I (A) - HENDAYE to ESTAVILLO

International Bridge   **0.0km**

Follow walkers' route to Church of Sta Maria.

To avoid steps, instead of turning right behind the Church of Sta Maria, continue straight on and turn right at the next road.

Irún   **1.4km**

Leave the Plaza de San Juan by Leon Iruratagoiena Kalea, to the right of the Town Hall (as you look at it), and head almost due south. Cross straight over a roundabout and keep straight on through a bridge under the Autopista to the district of Olaberria. Follow the road (GI-3452) parallel to a stream running down the valley, ignore all lanes which lead off to left and right and continue along it as it winds up the valley. After having travelled about 3.75kms in total, you will see a waste depot on your right and pass the point where the signed route joins the road you are on. Continue to

Gurrutze,   **7.5km**

Follow GI-2134 to

Oiartzun (Elizalde (C)).   **2.2km**

Turn left to go down past the museum and Church to the "plaza," and leave it by means of the road going off to the right to **Ugaldetxo,** and which almost immediately passes a road turning off to your right. Follow the GI-4532 straight across the crossroads in Ugaldetxo and up to join the GI-2132, which, by turning left along it, will lead you through the hills to

46

Astigárraga. 8.5km
Here, you join the road from San Sebastián, after which you can **either** follow
the walkers' route into Hernani over the 'new' Rio Urumea bridge, **or** follow the
route via Portu Auzoa/ El Puerto to bypass Hernani centre.
Hernani. 3.3km
Exit Plaza at SE corner and take the first turning on left after pedestrian steps
down to left. This will take you under the railway to El Puerto and on to
Urnieta. (by-passing Hernani centre) 2.5km
(via Hernani centre) 3.5km
Do not cross the bridge, but continue straight on, keeping the railway on your
right. Follow the road in front of the Kaiko works round the 'U' bend to the
right to cross over the railway tunnel and access the walkers' route. Follow it up
to the commercial premises, and continue on down to the GI-131, i.e. do not
turn left by the vehicle yard. Turn left along the GI-131, and then left again to
access the Industrial Estate service road.
It is thought not impossible to follow the waymarked walkers' route from here
all the way via
Andoain, 4.0km
Villabona and 5.5km
Anoeta to 4.0km
Tolosa. 2.8km
Follow Calle Gorosabel and Avenida de Araba out along the old N-1 to Venta
Aundi. Not long after, the road swings left under the new N-1. Turn right after
the bridge to follow the new cycle/pedestrian piste to
Alegia/Alegria de Oria, 4.7km
From here to Zegama it is necessary to follow the road routes, but, happily,
dedicated cycle lanes have been provided over much of the distance.
Legorreta, 5.8km
Ordizia, 5.0km
Beasain and 2.5km
Segura to 7.0km
Zegama. 5.1km
The GI-2637 continues from the Church in the town centre to start its long climb
towards the head of the valley.
Shortly the lane leading to the tunnel of San Adrián climbs off to the right to
start its journey over the Sierra de Urquilla, but unfortunately you will have to
stay with the road.
Your route, however, is very well graded and, although the incline is long, it
makes for very pleasant riding through the trees. In addition, there are some
quite exceptional views, especially that from a large rocky pinnacle, which is on
the left of the road as you approach the top of the pass, otherwise known as the

47

Puerto de Otzaurte. (Alt. 652m)   **8 0km**
Here, the very pleasant and helpful bar / restaurant is very welcome.
Continuing south from here, the main **N-1** has to be rejoined and great care has
to be exercised due to the gradient and the volume of traffic.
Follow the N-1 downhill and take the first available exit for
Alsasua (Altsasu (B)).   (To exit from N-1)   **5.5km**
Passage to Zalduondo was described to me in 2000 by the local Police and has
not been checked recently. Apologies are given for any discrepancy or error
found in the description.
Follow the exit road over the N-1 carriageways and into the town centre. Go
down the main street passing the Town Hall on your right. Follow this road
under a railway bridge and down to a T-junction (1.55kms), on the far right side
of which is a Restaurant. Follow the road round to the right and go past an N-1
access after 400m. The road will then take you over the A-240 and across two
roundabouts to **Olazti** (2.5kms). Fork right to travel the main street through the
town and go across the roundabout at its end to parallel the N-1 once more. You
will pass some factories on the way to another roundabout in front of a (?) hotel
and car park (3.8 kms).
Here, take the exit over the N-1 towards **Ziordia**, go 400m over the railway and
a stream and turn left. After 50m turn left again to follow Camino de Burunda to
Egin/Eguino (2.4kms). Follow the road through the village, and continue ahead
to pass through **Ilárduya** (2kms) and **Albéniz** (1.75kms). If you continue on and
go straight over the next crossroads, another 3.6kms will bring you to
Zalduondo.   **18.5km**
Now, you can rejoin the walkers' route by turning left immediately after the
church. You can follow it through
Ordoñana and   **3.0km**
Salvatierra to   **3.0km**
Gaceo.   **3.9km**
From here, you can make the recommended detour through Langarica and
Alaiza. (It is well worth it). If you do not, proceed directly through
Ezquerecocha to   (from Gaceo)   **2.0km**
Ermita de Nuestra Señora de Ayala.   **6.5km**
(You might have just completed the short detour to **Alegria**, which would have
made this section a little longer). From here, you continue on to
Elburgo   **3.0km**
and, perhaps, make the recommended detour to
Santuario de Nuestra Señora de Estíbaliz   **2.5km**
before continuing on to
Argandoña and   **1.1km**
Askartza/Ascarza.   **2.7km**
Continue along the **A-132/N-130**, turn left along the **N-104** at Elorriaga and at

the next roundabout go to the left of a filling station to follow **Portal de Elorriaga, Avda de Santiago and Portal del Rey** into the City centre. (Waymarks are in the pavement and not in the central *paseo*!!)

*To avoid the City Centre, proceed up **Portal de Elorriaga**, but turn left at a major junction with **Bulevar de Salburua**. Follow this, cross a roundabout, go under the railway and on to the elongated roundabout referred to in the Walkers' section. Go to its far end and turn right along **Venta de la Estrella**.*

Vitoria-Gasteiz. 5.5km

Follow the waymarked walkers' City Centre route out of the City.

(For an alternative route from Portal De Lasarte to Berantevilla, see later).

Armentia to (from the Centre) **3.5km**

Gomecha to **2.6km**

Subijana de Alava. **4.5km**

The N-1 valley route has to be used (see walkers' guide).

La Puebla de Arganzón. **9.5km**

Follow the walkers' route onto the N-1south but continue beyond the turn for Pangua etc and on to the next roundabout (near the service station).

Turn left for Burgueta. It is just beyond the bridge under the new A-1 that you rejoin, once again, the walkers' route.

Burgueta. **3.6km**

This section is passable in dry weather, but a little pushing may be involved.

Follow the track for the 2km to the 6-way crossroads. Here, instead of taking the walking route down the *Camino de los Peregrinos*, take the better surfaced road, to its left, which will veer left before it swings right to enter the top of

Estavillo (Estanillo(C), Estabelu (B)). **3.0km**

PART II (B) - ESTAVILLO to STO DOMINGO,

Refer now, to the Walkers' Route (P40/41), which will guide you to

Berantevilla. **5.5km**

Out of the village, do not turn left towards the cemetery but continue straight ahead for about 1.75km to the main road, where you turn left along the **N-124** and head south to

Zambrana. **4.3km**

Continue along the N-124, through the town (Julia's Bar on left).

Approximately 1.75km further on, you will see, on your left, the ruins of **Venta de Molino** and, very shortly after, the point where the walkers' route joins the road on which you are now travelling towards Salinillas.

Note The walkers' route to Salinillas is manageable but if you prefer tarmac surfaces, continue along the road, down past the service station / café / bar, and take the left turning further on, which is clearly signed to
Salinillas de Buradón (Buradón Gatzaga(B)). **6.0km**
The walkers' route does not lend itself to cyclists, so you should make your way back to the N-124 and turn left to go through the new road tunnel, constructed to facilitate traffic through the Conchas of Haro. When you reach **El Portal de la Rioja**, turn left along LR-132 to access
Briñas. Join and follow the walkers' route to **5.0km**
Haro, to the **motorway bridge** on the N-203. **3.7km**
It is recommends that, from here, you should continue to follow the road to Zarratón. However, if the ground is very dry, if your bicycle is very sturdy, and if you are not averse to a bit of pushing, you should be able to manage the walking route as far as the point where the track takes the left turn down the rutted cutting into the valley of the Rio Zamaca just before Zarratón. At this point, continue straight ahead, and you will come to a concrete piste leading down to the Casalarreina-Zarratón Road, where you turn left and follow the road into
Zarratón. **8.5km**
With care, the walking route should be manageable from here, but you have the alternative of following the road (south) via **Cidamón** and **San Torcuato** to
Bañares, (via road) **6.5km**
from where you take the road to

SANTO DOMINGO DE LA CALZADA. **4.5km**

PART II (C) - ESTAVILLO to BURGOS

I have no knowledge as to the viability of the walkers' route or of any other route as a practicable route for cyclists.

ALTERNATIVE CYCLISTS' ROUTE FROM VITORIA TO BERANTEVILLA

From the City Centre, follow the **Paseos Florida, Senda** *and* **Fray Francisco** *as far as the junction with Portal de Lasarte and Elvira Zulueta. Turn left down* **Portal de Lasarte,** *keep straight on at all intersections and follow the A-3102 towards Lasarte.*

If you have come along **Venta de la Estrella** *and the* **new paseo,** *you should turn left along the A-3102 road to Lasarte when you reach* **Portal de Lasarte.**

Keeping straight on at all intersections, go on through **Berrosteguieta** *and up through the Montes de Vitoria, where Wellington deployed his troops in the battle of Vitoria. You pass* **Doroño** *(on your left) after descending from the Montes, and you come to a junction with a road going off to the right.*

(The road to the right is a less used road and climbs up to and follows the crest of the hill as it passes through the tiny hamlets of Golernio, Busto de Treviño and Cucho on its way to the roundabout at its junction with the BU-744.)

The road straight on (now the BU-742) winds along the valley floor to meet the BU-741 in the vicinity of **Treviño,** *a hillside village with at least two bars. If you do not want to access Treviño on your left, turn right along the BU-741 towards La Puebla. After about 2km, you will reach a roundabout. Here, you turn left along the BU-744 (later to become the A-3122 / L-121) to*
Berantevilla *29.0km*

CYCLISTS' ROUTE from HARO to HERRAMÉLLURI
(With thanks to Eric Walker who devised the route)

This links up with the cycling route from Santo Domingo to Burgos, which is described in the Confraternity of St James' booklet, 'The Cycling Pilgrim on the Camino Francés'. If you follow this route, while you will miss out Sto Domingo, you will avoid much of the climbing through the Montes de Oca and still be able to visit San Juan de Ortega.

Haro
From the **Plaza Castañares de Rioja** take the **Avenida Sto Domingo** (to the right of the Bullring), and follow this road **(L-111)** to
Casalarreina, 6.0km
At the cross roads in Casalarreina go west along the **N-232** to
Tirgo. 3.5km
Do not swing right with the N-232 in the centre of the town, but go straight on along the **LR-201** and follow this road through **Cuzcurrita del Rio Tirón** and **Ochánduri** to reach the small town of
Herramélluri. 2.7km

ACKNOWLEDGEMENTS.

Special acknowledgement is given to Eric Walker who instigated the referencing of this route and provided early information with the help of Linda (Almeria University). I owe a debt of gratitude to Maria Teresa (Lizargarate), to José Ignacio (El Portal de la Rioja), to various officers of the Spanish Municipal Police, to Tourist Office assistants and to all those other people who have assisted with either direct or indirect contribution to or feedback on this guide. Nor must I forget (a) Manu and Sorkunde (Berango), who helped me compile the Glossary below, and (b) my walking companion, Judith Leigh, who helped me gather information for and proof-walk this guide.

The Author acknowledges and thanks the authors and publishers of the following books, publications, leaflets and web sites to which reference has been made, and whose content has helped in the production of this Guide:

Dos Caminos a Santiago	Carlos Pérez de Uralde, J.A.Lecanda y N.Azurmendi. Published by Dept de Comercio, Consumo y Turismo del Gobierno Vasco.
El Camino de Santiago	Mercedes Reig. Published by Turespaña, Secretaria General de Turismo.
Por Álava a Compostela en Las Rutas de Europa	Alfonso Maria Abella and Garcia de Eulate. Published by Dpt de Cultura, Diputacion Foral de Alava.
The Santiago Way through The Basque Country.	Fernando Imaz. Published by the Autonomous Community of Euskadi.
Hendaye	l'Abbé Michelena. Publisher unknown. Text supplied by Bibliotheque Hendaye.
Guia de Pequeños Hoteles y Alojamientos en el Medio Rural *Michelin Guide to Spain*	Published by Los Departamentos de Industria Comercio y Turismo de los Diputaciones Forales de Alava, Bizkaia y Gipuzkoa

Asociación Amigos del Camino de Mirando de Ebro

www.mundicamino.com

MAPS
Michelin Map No. 442

Mapa Provincial 1:200,000.de   Published by Centro Nacionál de
Álava, Guipúzcoa and Vizcaya   Información Geográfica (CNIG)

IGN   **www.sigpac.mapa.es/fega/visor**
can be navigated to inspect and/or copy
maps up to 1:20000 scale and satellite
pictures at larger scales.

Maps are available from: The Map Shop,
15 High Street, Upton-on- Severn,
Worcestershire, WR8 0HJ
Tel. 01684 593146
Fax. 01684 594559

GLOSSARY OF BASQUE WORDS:

Basque lands (Navarre + three Fr provinces)	Euskal Herria
I'm sorry; I do not understand Euskera	Barkátu, ez dut Euskéraz ulértzen
Pardon / excuse me	Barkatu
Hello	(Kaixo (polite),
	(Áupa or Épa (familiar)
Goodbye	Agúr
See you later	Geroárte
Until we meet again	Uréngoárte
Please	Mesédez
(No)Thank you	(Ez) Eskérrik ásko
Don't mention it.	Ez dágo zeráitik
Yes	Bai
No	Ez
How are you?	Zer modúz
Very well thank you. And you?	Óndo or Óngi. Éta zu?
Welcome	Óngi etórri
Good morning / afternoon	Egunón
Good afternoon / evening	Arrátsaldéon
Goodnight	Gabón
Sleep well	Óndo ló egín

Bon voyage	Ondo ibíli
And to you.	Álan ekárri
Bar	Tabérna (Edaritégi)
Bar/Restaurant	Jatetxéa
Cider bar	Sagardotégi
Toilets	Kómunak
Water	Úra
Milk	Ésnea
Coffee (white)	Káfe esnéa
Coffee (black)	Káfe útsa
Coffee (with little milk)	Káfe ebákia
Cider	Sagárdo
Beer (in bottle)	Garagárdo
Beer (draught)	Káña
Beer (v small glass)	Zuríto
Wine	Árdo
Glass of red wine	Ardo beltza
Fountain	Iturria
The water is (not) drinkable	Ur (ez) édarjerría/édajarría
Drinking this water is not good for you	Ur edaritek itxarra
Bon appetit	Ón egín
Breakfast	Gosári
Lunch	Bazkari
Dinner	Afári
Meat	Haragi
Chicken	Óillo
Ham	Úrdaiázpikóa
Pork	Txerríki
Beef	Behíki
Fish	Arraina
Omelette	Tortilla
Chips	Frijítuak
Stew	Sálda
Bread	Ogía
Bakery	Akindegi
Cheese	Gázta
Egg	Árrautz
House	Etxe
Large house	Caserío
Palacio / Manor House / Farmhouse	Jauregi
Hostel	Aterpéa
Hotel/Hostal	Ostátua

Cross	Gurutzé
Church	Elíza
Street	Kalé
Road, path or trail	Bidé
District	Auzóa
River (large) / (small)	Ibaia / Erréka
Mountain	Mendi
Valley	Larran
Health Centre	Osasún Zentrua
Red Cross	Gurútze Górria
Tourist Office	Turísmoa Bulegóa
Town Hall	Údaletxéa
Municipal Police	Údaltzaingoa
(Old) City centre	Hirigúne (historikoa).

Contact address for feedback, comments, corrections and suggested amendments

C. A. Roberts
19 Linacre Rd
Eccleshall
Staffordshire ST21 6DZ

Email: tony.roberts19@tiscali.co.uk

Tel: 01785 850514

I will be happy to try to answer any queries about or to give further assistance in connection with this route insofar as I am able. In return I should be grateful for any feedback, which would help me to keep this guide up to date.
Tony Roberts, March 2010

Page left blank for notes.

NATALIA
38 Rue Ramoy
75018